MAINE'S
GOLDEN
ROAD

Happy 81, Dad!
♡
love ♡
♡ Elizabeth

Books by John Gould

New England Town Meeting
Pre-natal Care for Fathers
Farmer Takes a Wife
The House That Jacob Built
And One to Grow On
Neither Hay nor Grass
Monstrous Depravity
The Parables of Peter Partout
You Should Start Sooner
Last One In
Europe on Saturday Night
The Jonesport Raffle
Twelve Grindstones
The Shag Bag
Glass Eyes by the Bottle
This Trifling Distinction
Next Time Around
No Other Place
Stitch in Time
The Wines of Pentagoët
Old Hundredth
There Goes Maine!
Funny about That
It Is Not Now
Dispatches from Maine—1942–1992
Maine's Golden Road

With F. Wenderoth Saunders
The Fastest Hound Dog in the State of Maine

With Lillian Ross
Maine Lingo

MAINE'S
GOLDEN
ROAD

A Memoir

(On the 31st of August, 1846, I left Concord in Massachusetts for Bangor and the backwoods of Maine. . . .
—*Henry David Thoreau*)

A second opinion about a couple of million acres of the Great North Maine Wilderness 150 years after the Philosopher of Walden Pond carried an umbrella to the top of his beloved Mount Ktaadn

---

JOHN GOULD

W.W. Norton & Company • New York • London

And for Grandson Tom's Bride

BRIJETTA

First Edition

The text of this book is composed in Bembo.
Composition and manufacturing by The Maple-Vail Book Manufacturing Group.

ISBN: 978-0-393-34936-8

W. W. Norton & Company, Inc., 500 Fifth Avenue, New York, N.Y. 10110
W. W. Norton & Company Ltd., 10 Coptic Street, London WC1A 1PU

1 2 3 4 5 6 7 8 9 0

PETER PARTOUT'S PAGE

Dear Mr. Editor: This Vermonter, Bill Dornbusch,
is a decent chap just the same.

(Signed)   Peter Partout
                        Peppermint Corner

From *The Length and Breadth of Maine*
by Stanley B. Attwood
Augusta, 1946

PC4 Caucomagomac Lake. 7R15, 6R15,
7R14, and 6R14, WELS. Length 6.5
miles. Area 7.0 Sq. m. Previous desig-
nations, Caucomagamook, St. John
Lake (MJC), Caucomgomoc (GR1).
Also Caucomagomuc, Caucomago-
mak, Kahmoguamook.

(Pronounced *kok-m'gommick*. Locally, ab-
breviated to *kok*. i.e.—Cauc Lake, Cauc
Landing, Cauc Dam, Cauc Stream.)

MAINE'S
GOLDEN
ROAD

COMMENCE HERE:

A Dr. Georg Dietrich was editor of the *Taunus Anzeiger,* a small newspaper in the village of Oberursel, not far from Frankfurt, in Germany. In 1960 the United States invited him to come and see our country, with the thought that he might write some words to promote international goodwill. For ten days Dr. Dietrich inspected the airports of Boston, New York, Chicago, Miami, Philadelphia, Washington, Dallas, Seattle, Los Angeles, and Atlanta. Then he flew back to Germany. His book appeared in three weeks, and the title was *Das Ist Amerika.*

In 1846 Henry David Thoreau left his microcosmic Concord by the Boston boat to come down to Maine to look things over and in particular climb Mount Katahdin, for which he used the Indian form, Ktaadn. Twice, later, he came again to canoe Chesuncook Lake and the Penobscot River's West Branch, a portion of the Allagash River, and the East Branch of the Penobscot. His three visits came to about a month. His book *The Maine Woods* remained in journal form until posthumously published.

Bill and I have made annual excursions into the country

Thoreau visited for thirty summers, now camping where he
camped, and even disporting with the *Chimaphila maculata*
where he was prone to pluck. You can say we picked Thoreau's rear.

Felix Fernald, a woods clerk for Great Northern Paper
Company all his life, was stationed for a long time at Pittston
Farm. In lumber camp lingo a "farm" is a depot and base of
operations serving a considerable area of working timberland. Pittston Farm had storage sheds, garages, hay barns and
horse stables, sleeping and eating quarters, office space, and
the telephone exchange over which Felix's wife, Velma, prevailed. Great Northern also had Grant's Farm, Michaud
Farm, and others. Partly for his own amusement and partly
for company documentation Felix mimeographed from time
to time his *Pittston Farm News*. Here is an excerpt from the
issue of June 3, 1966: "The rear of North Branch Drive
passed through Big Bog Dam on May 30, a little later than
last year. It should be into the deadwater today or tomorrow.
The South Branch Drive rear went through Canada Falls
Dam on May 31, but the rear is very heavy and it will no
doubt take another week to get into Seboomook deadwater."

Thoreau came in summer and early fall and never saw a
Maine river in spring with its drive of logs. And Bill and I,
in July, didn't—although Bill and I did see stranded wood
still being "picked" and tossed back in the streams, and at
Seboomook Lake they were still using "boomjumpers" to
pick the rear. A boomjumper was a powerboat with shielded
propeller so it could pass without damage among floating
logs. But river driving had ceased. The environmentalists
take some credit for this, but in truth the decision to build
all-season roads and turn to trucks had been made by the
timberland owners before the cleanup agitation began.
Maine's "Golden Road" had already been many years on the
engineer's drawing board.

So "picking Thoreau's rear" is just a manner of speaking.
Bill and I found it great fun.

HOW BIG IS A MOOSE?

> The mission of man there seems to be like so many busy
> demons, to drive the forest all out of the country, from
> every solitary beaver swamp and mountain side, as soon
> as possible.
>
> —*Thoreau upon first approaching the
> Maine Woods in 1846*

In early afternoon of the thirty-first of August in that good year
of 1846, a man not yet acquainted with age stepped from the
woodland trail to Walden Pond and adjusted his pace to the
sophisticated village street of his beloved Concord, Maffa-
chuffets. He was warmly dressed for a bright late-summer
day, and he carried a rough valise, or sack, that suggested he
might be starting a journey. Indeed, before he turned down
the town road towards Boston, he paused to look back at the
village—as if making an inward adieu at a scene he wanted
to retain in his memory. Mother Mabel Crowthers, a Con-
cordian of inquisitive leanings who knew this young man
well, was close by, and she said: "Good day to you, Master
Henry—have you been away?"

Thus Henry David Thoreau, the sage of Concord and the
philosopher of Walden Pond, forsook his limited vistas and
came by railroad and steamboat to the District of Maine,
where he would make early, and literary, comments on the
Maine Woods, and also climb Mount Katahdin, which he
spelled Indian fashion—Ktaadn. Mr. Thoreau was then
twenty-nine years of age and although a graduate of Harvard

College was considered fairly bright. His destiny was to answer the request of Ralph Waldo Emerson for a literate American. The Maine Woods made an excellent place to start.

But we must face it—there has to be something quirky when any graduate of Harvard College goes mountain climbing. I never climbed Katahdin, having attended a lesser college, but I did climb Mount Abraham once, being inveigled, or swindled, into the stunt by some friends *sans merci.* "Oh!" they teased. "Would not this be a happy weekend to venture to the top of Mount Katahdin?"

"I am all tied up with the cribbage tournament," I improvised.

My wife said, "That was last week."

I said, "Fact is, Katahdin's no fun this time of year anyway; it's overrun with Boy Scouts who are kind, loyal, trustworthy, reverent, and clean, and they keep helping us registered guides over blowdowns. I'll break a rule and take you up Mount Abraham. The height's about the same."

We did climb Mount Abraham (4,040 feet) and at the top we looked down on beautiful Maine and somebody said, "OOOOOOOH! Isn't that lovely down there!"

I said it certainly was, and if they'd excuse me, I'd go back down and enjoy it.

In Thoreau's time, not too many people had gone up Katahdin. The Indians, seemingly, were superstitious about Pomola, the spirit of the peak, who was jealous unless you brought him a bottle of rum. Empty bottles didn't count. My better guess is that the untutored savage was smarter than a good many folks supposed. The Indian guide that Thoreau engaged protested that he hadn't even climbed Mount Kineo—eighteen hundred feet. Neither have I. Exercise is best from a sedentary posture.

Eager to be off into the woods, Henry David Thoreau three times neglected to dwell on the joy of a trip from Boston to Bangor by steamship. Bangor was already a thriving city of many thousand people, the largest lumber center in

America. Cargoes of forest products left by every tide for the far places of the world—and brought back comforts and delights to adorn life and living. Truly on the edge of the wilderness, Bangor enjoyed cates and dainties fetched home to make the title "Queen City" mean something. But while lumber, and goodies, came and went by brigs and barques, there was also a fleet of profitable steamships in Thoreau's time making convenient overnight voyages from Boston Down East to Portland, Bath, Rockland, and Bangor. Soon larger vessels would be added to extend the service to St. John and Halifax; the Maritimes had many sons and daughters in the "Boston States."

Pity, then, that Henry Thoreau paid so little attention to the trim white steamer that carried him out of Boston Harbor on that pleasant afternoon; the steamers were a novelty among the sailing craft he would meet and pass on the voyage. And unless nasty weather blew up, the voyage was smooth and scenic. Leaving Boston Harbor in late afternoon, the boat offered a handsome sunset over Arlington Heights as she changed course to move past Cape Ann towards the never-never land of Down East. There was always somebody aboard to point at the Reef of Norman's Woe and recite about the *Hesperus*. Evening arrived, and the lighthouses of the Maine perked up one by one: Isles of Shoals, the Nubble, and after Portland Head Light the triple delight of Halfway Rock, Seguin, and rugged Monhegan. There, at Monhegan, the Pilgrims first saw America—and first saw Maine. But before coming this far, the passenger tidies in his stateroom (two dollars extra) and appears for supper, making shipmate friends and watching the sea to starboard and the dark green hills of Maine to port. Thoreau, however, explicit about every observation once he steps ashore, tells us about his voyage Down East wholly in terms of the vexatious steward who comes to disturb his slumber and his meditations, inquiring if he would like to have his shoes shined.

In Bangor Thureau continues to ignore important matters and right away begins to castigate the evil lumberers with

their vicious axes. Not one word, for instance, about breakfast at the Penobscot Exchange Hotel.

In Thoreau's time, Bangor certainly worked both ends of
the street. The timber barons had magnificent homes and
already had begun endowing the finest public library in
Maine. Bangor had its society and Bangor had wealth—in
timberlands, in industry, and in ships at sea. Bangor also had
daring and heroic woodsmen who came to town at the end
of every spring drive and sought amusement, retiring only
when their season's earnings were spent. The tidal end of
Exchange Street came to be known as the Devil's Half Acre,
and things went on there that genteel Bangorians chose to
live with. There came to be in time, for instance, the gracious
lady Fan Jones, who had a standing in community affairs
when other less understanding towns would have disdained
her. Once a year Fan Jones would adorn the lovely young
ladies of her court with the most lavish gowns the Parisian
couturiers could provide, expense being no object, and Fan
would install them in an open coach-and-six to ride in the
gala parade for the opening of Bangor State Fair. A large tent
had been set up for the week's engagement. And halfway
of the Devil's Half Acre stood Bangor's leading hotel—the
Penobscot Exchange. Thoreau is silent on this.

The boat from Boston could land its passengers in Portland, Bath, and Rockland for a timely breakfast, but even
with a coming tide it took longer to Bangor, so it would be
ten or eleven o'clock before the hungry voyagers hustled
from the city landing up Exchange Street to invade the
Exchange. The kitchen and dining room were quite ready.
Breakfast was thirty-five cents. This included the porridge,
with molasses and cream, the steak and eggs with hashbrown
potatoes, a serving of turnip, hot cream-tartar biscuits or
johnnycake, pancakes with maple syrup, a side dish of logging berries (known as baked beans in Boston) with the
choice of pie, and coffee or tea (boiled).

Forever uncelebrated by Henry David Thoreau, the
Devil's Half Acre and the Penobscot Exchange went their
way in an urban renewal project of our more enlightened

age. It's difficult to pass that way today and imagine wood-choppers disporting their frolics, to suppose that this is where the high-steppin' horses took the girls to work, that just down there the gleaming white Boston boat whistled its morning arrival—and that breakfast cost thirty-five cents.

Thoreau's departure from Bangor didn't take long—perhaps because he missed so much. He went directly to Stillwater and Old Town, where he found a guide, laid in his supplies, and took to the woods. He said he was impatient to see a moose, and that's how we learn that he carried an umbrella when he climbed Mount Katahdin. Bill and I are certainly not the first to be amused by this intrusion of a civilized convenience into the joys of rugged adventure—although let us not forget that an early requirement of Robinson Crusoe was his bumbershoot. Thoreau revealed that when it came time to measure his first moose, he lacked a yardstick and was obliged to make his scientific sizes in umbrella sections.

A seasoned Maine woodsman does not usually carry an umbrella. Back in the early days of the L. L. Bean mail-order business, when a lah-di-dah element first began to appear north of Ogunquit, Mr. Bean condescended and offered a waterproof foul-weather cape that had the usual unconditional Bean guarantee and came in an oilskin pouch about the size of a man's wallet. Tucked in a pocket, it weighed little and took little space. The thing did have a fault. If a shower came up, the unfolded garment kept the customer dry as advertised, but when the sun reappeared, there was no possible way to refold the thing and put it back in the little pouch. The packing secret was known only to the manufacturer. Try as he did, every customer either left his L. L. Bean rain gear hanging on a spruce limb somewhere beyond Lily Bay or stuffed it in a hundred-pound feed bag and sent it to Freeport to get his money back. Mr. Bean's unqualified money-back pledge cost him dearly, and the item was not in the next catalog. His buyers did, however, find other weather gear, but there is still something to be said for an umbrella if you expect to measure a moose.

INTRODUCING WILLIAM

> He was a verray, parfit gentil knight.
> —*Geoffrey Chaucer*

Bill Dornbusch knows everything in a pleasant and congenial way.

Years ago there lived over towards North Monmouth a gentleman of advertised erudition, and we always smiled as we passed his farm. His large-size rural free delivery postbox by the road was conspicuously lettered thus:

REGINALD FREDERICK MONTREFORT, Ph.D.

His fields were lush, his cattle sleek, his buildings in repair, and there was no reason to snicker except that modest Maine folks, even if they have any, do not flaunt their academic honors on their sleeves or on their mailboxes. Which is to say that while Bill is a Mainer only by osmosis, he is versed well enough in the basic amenities to keep his great knowledge from rendering him obnoxious to us common sort.

Bill and I share two grandsons. We became acquainted during the early days of the relevant courtship, and when his comely daughter persuaded my ne'er-do-well son to wed, Bill and I decided things had gone far enough for us to pay attention and for us to become serious friends. While grandparentage was still incipient, Bill and I organized our first "Grandfathers' Retreat," and with the enthusiasms of youth and health, and a copy of *The Maine Woods* by Henry David

Thoreau, we disappeared for a glorious week far above Canada Falls, even above the brave West Branch of the Penobscot River, and we tented in the serenity of our own meditations exactly where the outlet of Baker Lake donates the first drops of clear mountain springwater into the St. John River. We were twenty miles from the Canadian boundary at the French-speaking village of Ste.-Aurélie, Quebec. Since then Bill and I have made thirty consecutive retreats into the very townships Thoreau came to know, but perhaps never so well as we.

The Great West Branch timberlands are much larger than Bill's whole Republic of Vermont, where Bill lives in retirement at Bennington—tuition at Bennington College is said to be exorbitantly impressive. But he did have some knowledge of Maine. He'd bring his family for summer outings, first to the perch and bass pond at North Monmouth and then to Kennebago Lake, far up in the trout and salmon country. But these visits could not be considered "tenting out" and were to recreational areas rather than to the Maine wilderness.

Bill's father came to New York City as an immigrant from the great Hanseatic State of Bremen. His *Fleisch* and *Feinkost* shop prospered, and Bill grew up a city kid and the son of the German butcher. German was then his first language. But by the time I met Bill he said he had forgotten his German—something I found was not quite so if I tossed an odd German word at him. Caught unawares, he'd toss one back. Today there is no trace of the Teutonic in Bill's speech, but I think we can rightly say there is a trace of the North German in his stature and his appearance. Dornbusch is still a common family name around Stadtbremen, and Bill has relatives down in that other storied wilderness the Black Forest.

The reason Bill is so smart is explained by his profession: He was a reporter in the Surrogate Court of Westchester County, New York State, taking records of trials and of pretrial conferences. Whenever he was assigned to a case, he would methodically retire and do his homework. It is not

seemly if a reporter, in an exciting context, interrupts to ask
a witness how to spell "pedunculate." In this way Bill filled
his receptive noggin until he was the perfect example of Vol-
taire's "gentleman"—one who prides himself on nothing. No
specialist, Bill, I've never known a subject to arise and find
him speechless, and he's not one to list his erudition on his
mailbox.

There came a summer when our son was headwaiter and
bartender at the Kennebago Lake Club, and Bill's daughter
had been promoted from a paying guest to a waitress. Bill
was pleasantly affected by a Manhattan that seemed better
than others, and since nobody with a good Manhattan recipe
goes blabbing it about, chicanery prevailed and it wasn't long
before the engagement was announced and Bill was adding a
splash of maple syrup to his cocktail.

In 1991 the Department of Archaeology and Paleontology of
the Caucomagomac Dam Institute of Fine and Coarse Art
uncovered a fossil tusk of an Ice Age mastodon in a dig at
Township 8, Range 15, near St. Francis Lake. Professor Dornbusch is here seen lecturing on the importance of the find.
Radiocarbon dating fixes the age of the beast at twelve thousand years. This is the first evidence that *Mammut americanum*
ever roamed the North Maine Woods. Professor Dornbusch
estimates the animal, when alive, measured six umbrellas in
length and stood five umbrellas high at the shoulder.

I believe Bill's upgrading from a dilettante summercater to
an informed philosopher of the Maine Woods came with an
introduction to a lady sport I was guiding at Kennebago. She
was from Huntington, New York, and fished only for trout
with dry Parmacheenee Belle flies she tied herself—using a
three-ounce Thomas bamboo rod. She had asked Bill to
name his favorite trout fly. In less time than it takes a judge
to cry "Order in the Court," Bill was an expert on artificial
lures and began telling about cow dungs and wullff grasshop-
pers. He was ready for the big time.

We did need a pass over both Great Northern and International Paper roads to reach Baker Lake, and friends in both companies favored us. The campsite we used was open to the public but meant for canoe parties in the St. John rather than motorists coming by logging roads. From the beginning Bill and I knew we were privileged and very lucky to know the right people. In thirty years Bill and I have not had to share our campsite with Boy Scouts, and only a couple of times with anglers seeking the muskelunge found in Maine only at Baker Lake. The State of Maine keeps two good camps at the outlet—one as shelter to an occasional game warden working the district, and another for forest rangers moved in during dry times. You can say that Bill and I own the place.

But the remote parts of the deep woods, with just two random interlopers encouraging the scenery, can become busy-busy and surprise you with improbable activity. One year the United States Border Patrol moved in an aluminum house trailer that intruded on the ten thousand acres Bill and I held in full possession, and an interlude began. Two handsome gentlemen in what might have been Knights Templars regalia for the quarter days came and went in stately measure as if seeking something that could not be found. A third gentleman, in spotless white, busied himself within, and he proved to be the expedition's cook. Shortly a magnificent pall of pan-fried onions pervaded the sylvan scene, and caused Bill and me great confusion, as we had been planning on camp fries at suppertime, not at noon.

We inquired discreetly, without hampering any of the official programming, and learned some "bonds" were misplaced and if found would be dealt with the full impact of international law. After two nights the trailer was gone, and one of the International Paper scalers told us a bond was a French-Canadian working in Maine who had posted a bond as security for his whereabouts. He said bonds are mighty hard to catch in that country. We heard that one bond who hadn't been caught was working as cook in the trailer.

Another time a forest ranger and his wife came to open the shed and test all the fire equipment. They spread hose up and

down the riverbank, set up an electric pump, oiled all the
Indian pumps, and, after deciding that all systems were go,
they washed a beautiful Newfoundland dog that was a perfect slob and loved every squirt.

The quickest way to reach our Baker Lake preserve is
straight up the road from Skowhegan, Maine, through Jackman to the Canadian border at Armstrong. Then you shift to
metrics and go about forty kilometers to the considerable city
of St. Georges, Beauce County, Quebec. In that short distance you have left everything Yankee behind and are not
only in a different land but in a completely different culture.
A short ride to the small village of Ste.-Aurélie fetches you
smack against the customs gate, beyond which is the State of
Maine. The gate is open for limited hours on certain days,
and a passport from our Department of State will do you no
good. The beautiful logging road of the International Paper
Company is the only access to that part of Maine, and if you
are on any kind of proper woodland business, you will have
a pass that lets you through. It is vexing to some uninformed
tourists when they see "foreign" Canadians zip through, but
get a big NO themselves in spite of Massachusetts and Connecticut license plates. The happy exception are Bill and I,
who still keep our signed passes handy, but enjoy the higher
honor after all these years of a wave and a nod. But thirty
years ago, when Bill and I first visited Baker Lake, we came
north from Moosehead Lake, by Twenty Mile and Pittston
Farm, and straight along the Rainey Brook logging road—a
route shortly abandoned. But we do try to get over to Ste.-
Aurélie for the fun of a visit, and some merry times have
ensued. Ste.-Aurélie is a frolic spot for most of the folks now
in charge of Thoreau's Maine Woods.

COUNT ME IN!

From Kittery to Fort Kent, from Eastport to the Magalloway, I have traveled well in Maine—the length and breadth.

—*John Gould*

My fetchin-up was not at all like Bill's. Our town of Freeport, in Maine, had "about" twenty-five hundred folks, but that included South Freeport, the saltwater harbor. We lived "not quite" in the village in a big "sea captain's" home with enough land so we had gardens, apple trees and berry bushes, hens, a cow, pigs, and honeybees. Over our back lot line we stepped directly into heavy spruce woods. Mr. L. L. Bean, whose mail-order business would soon make little Freeport world-renowned, was, in my youth, just another main street storekeeper, selling gents' wear and Walk-Over Shoes in partnership with his brother Guy. Near enough so I spent considerable time with him, my grandfather had a real farm with a barnful of cattle and whole fields in crops.

Freeport had a seafaring heritage, and half the older gentlemen in town had been all over the world with the great "down easters" of the latter 1800s, so it was a town where boys learned to box the compass well before they were spelling big words. Our high school, which I negotiated with a third-place graduation essay, did offer four years of Latin, which I "took," but lacked certain refinements now considered essential—drama, soccer, band, baton twirling, and so on. My father warned me that the teachers would likely try to steer me towards shorthand and typing, but if I took the languages, history, and maybe some laboratory stuff, I'd probably wind up prosperous enough to hire all the stenographers I'd need.

When I was thirteen, it came to my attention that my several playmates had Daisy BB rifles, and because I didn't I was missing many adventures. I asked if I could have a BB gun. My father dismissed the matter in no uncertain terms. No weapon, he said, is meant to be a toy, and a BB gun is dangerous. More eyes have been put out, he said, by BB guns than by all the keyholes in every cheap hotel in America. I could damn well forget it. My father was not otherwise hard to get along with, so I forgot it. But that October, on my fourteenth birthday, he beckoned me from the kitchen into the shed, and he handed me a brand-new Winchester single-shot .22 rifle. Taking a box of cartridges from his pocket, he suggested we step out behind the buildings and study ballistics. It requires some thoughtful adjustment to understand why a BB gun is dangerous, but a .22 rifle, which can kill a moose, is suitable for a fourteen-year-old boy. I will add here that I have never been a member of the National Rifle Association.

When Mr. L. L. Bean heard that I had acquired a .22, he went out of his way to invite me to join him and his friends for a few targets in the basement of his store. But I never did have a Daisy air gun. My dad taught me how to whistle a snowshoe rabbit, and then how to dress it and skin it so Mother could make us a pie, and also how to get a couple of old hens ready for Sunday dinner. He taught me to graft an apple tree and how to set a hen and how to hive a swarm of bees. He took me to the brook for my first trout, and I'll never forget the time he "lost" me in the woods on purpose and then watched to see if I'd paid attention to his instructions. I had, and when at last he appeared (from another direction), I looked up to say, "You did that a-purpose!" That first day in the woods with my new birthday gun, he set a horse chestnut in the crotch of a tree and let me have four shots—two worked. Then he supervised cleaning the gun, and cleaning the gun, and cleaning the gun. . . . I learned sure enough how to clean the gun. And because I took care of it, I still have it.

My father also taught me to skin my own skunks, something recommended in an old Maine adage. There is no great talent needed to catch a skunk: If you set a trap under a box in the middle of a forty-acre field, a skunk will find some way to spring the trap. And as a prime skunk pelt in my obnoxious youth would bring fifty cents from the Friend Hide & Fur Company, most boys had a trapline and stunk like the devil in school. Many's the day Miss Loring, our grammar school principal, sent one of us to fetch Mr. Deering, the janitor, to bring his long window pole and vent the classrooms. But after my first skunk, my father showed me how to take the scented beast, trap and all, to the brook and tie him so the flowing water eased away the passion. Two days did the trick, and I could skin my skunk without troubling Mr. Deering.

My occasional visits to Grandfather's farm were always instructive. Gramp had been a volunteer in Company I, Sixteenth Maine Regiment, and when he learned that I now owned a .22 rifle, he said, "When you're a mite bigger," he'd let me shoot the musket he had carried the first day at Gettysburg. Given to him at mustering out in 1865, he used the musket on crows and hawks and woodchucks that abused his farming. Instead of a Civil War ball, he used a handful of shot. When he did let me shoot it, at a target, it knocked me flat in the dooryard. Grandfather never belonged to the National Rifle Association either.

Best fun with Gramp was lunchtime in his woodlot. He had a forty-acre firewood lot about four miles from his farmhouse, and as soon as there was snow enough, he'd take the team and the sled, and a lunch, and begin harvesting the next year's fuel. During his war the Sixteenth Maine was part of the "Blanket Brigade" which you can find in some of the history books. The War Department "lost" five regiments,

and for months no supply wagons approached. The men for-
aged for food and in time resorted to wrapping their blankets
about them for both warmth and modesty. My grandfather
became sort of official forager for his company and as a farm
boy was able to "liberate" animals and dress them out. He
told me how he came upon some cavalry officers who had
just slaughtered a milch cow somewhere in "dirty Virginia"
and they had no notion of how to make the crittur ready for
the stewpot. Grandfather, then a lad of eighteen, offered to
cut up the animal if they would give him the head. He told
me, "I contrived to bring the head away so a good part of the
forequarters came with it." That evening Company I dined
well.

Gramp would build a small campfire when we first came
to the woodlot, citing the Indian warning "Little fire, get
warm; big fire, freeze to death," and our basket of lunch was
disposed so things wouldn't freeze. The horses were tied to
two trees, shoulder to shoulder, and hay thrown down to
entertain them. Then we'd cut wood, and I had my boy's ax,
until the sun was over the big beech tree. Then the old soldier
would give the horses a drink from the brook, attach their
nose bags with oats, and cook up a banquet. He'd use one of
the horse pails as a reflector oven and bring off biscuits you
wouldn't believe.

Evening comes early in a winter woodlot, so we'd load
the sled in due time and let the horses have their heads for the
trip home. On these outings I was expected to spend the
night with Gramp at the farm, so after some popcorn and a
pan of apples he'd light me up to an unheated chamber,
where a feather tick and several "comfortables" had been
cooling for me since the last time. I'd shiver myself to sleep,
and the next thing I knew Gramp would be at the foot of the
stairs, calling up to me from the open door of the warm
kitchen, "I'm off to the barn to chore up; you stay a-bed
long's you want to and breakfast is on the stove!"

Maybe I should have explained that Gramp, in my boyhood, lived alone so I always had him all to myself.

THE INSTITUTE

> When the state wishes to endow an academy or a university, it grants it a tract of forest land: one saw represents an academy; a gang [of saws] a university.
>
> —*Thoreau, philosophizing along the*
> *East Branch about the depredations to the*
> *Maine woodlands in the desire for culture*

When Bill and I realized that our early visitations to the North Maine Woods were extending themselves into a substantial series, we decided an effort should be made to emphasize that we had been there; we should (like the Athenian plebes) do something to improve the situation. It was shameful to think that well over a century had passed since Henry David Thoreau had tented this way, and nothing remained to recall his visits. His Harvard perspicacity didn't show. And our laudable desire to bring some kind of cultural nicety to the wilderness was supported by our need for something to do. Every summer, when we got home, our several friends would question us on our activities. "How can you two stand a whole week of doing nothing up in that wasteland?" they would say, and we needed an answer.

It bothered us that here were these millions of acres of uninhabited land completely devoid of cultural refinements and the gracious attributes of learning. Not an academy and not a university; not a single public library beyond Greenville! Not even postal service to bring correspondence classes from the Franklin Institute or bulletins from the Extension

Service. So Bill and I founded the Caucomogomac Dam
Institute of Fine and Coarse Art, and with full cooperation
from the several landowners this academic innovation was an
immediate success. Every summer we have brought lectures,
seminars, and philosophic opportunities to the region, and
then, when we go home at the conclusion of our erudite pro-
grams, we can tell our friends just what we do up there.

It was incredible that television, even, did not intrude into
the destitute area. We did take a portable radio with us, but
there was no broadcasting station to reach us save one in St.
Georges, Quebec, which offered only replays of last season's
ice hockey games, in French. After one July of this we took
a tape player and had a little Brahms and Victor Herbert as
preludes to our evening study sessions. Bill himself is keen
on history, and for his introductory effort he presented his
usual three-hour lecture on "Washington's Generals." Lacking electricity, however, he couldn't present his accompa-
nying lantern slides. To show the quality of his presentation
here is the text of his remarks at our crepuscular convocation
on the fourteenth of July, A.D. 1988:

> Paper delivered in general auditorium of the Cau-
> comgomac Dam Institute of Fine and Coarse Art,
> Township 6, Range 14, by Professor Dornbusch, De-
> partment of Fractured History, in observance of the
> anniversary of the storming of the Bastille, July 14,
> 1789, on July 14, 1988.

> Dr. Dornbusch:

> Mr. Provost, Chairman and Members, Board of
> Trustees, Distinguished Overseers, Fellow Faculty,
> Directors of Institutional Coordination, Visiting Dig-
> nitaries and Associate Professors, Representatives of
> Sister Institutions, Your Excellency:
> History, long acknowledged as the foremost of
> docents, often admonishes us with erroneous informa-

tion and sleazy facts. Such is the case with the Bastille, that former fortress and prison so revered and venerated in the annals of the Republic of France—the raison d'être of our present assemblage at this time, right now, presently. We are gathered here at this moment to offer memorial tribute to that edifice, presuming it to be what History has said it was for lo! these many years. [Applause.] Truth, with which History brooketh no fellowship, tells another tale.

Instead of a venerable symbol of bigotry, cruelty, royal caprice and tyranny, incarcerating great numbers of oppressed and abused citizens, enduring since its completion in the eleventh century during the reign of Charles V, known as Charles the Wise, it was, instead, an obsolete, antiquated relic of no particular significance. Let me digress with an amusing anecdote about King Charles V.

When Charles was a small boy, a chum of his stole two peaches in a nearby orchard and offered one of them to the prince, who began at once to eat it. The chum, meantime, went to a brook and carefully washed the other peach before he ate it. To him, the future King Charles V said, "My dear boyhood chum, why do you so assiduously cleanse your peach while I, of royal blood and one day to rule France, am less particular?"

Whereat the boyhood chum replied, "Sire, one of my peaches fell onto the dung heap, and I wist not which one it was!" And ever after that, King Charles V always had his peaches washed, and was called the Wise. But let us return to *nos moutons*.

During the infamous time of Cardinal Richelieu the fortress Bastille housed the victims of his lettres de cachet, who, without trial, were imprisoned at the cardinal's whim, usually for no crime at all. Those days had long passed, but the people of Paris, needing excuses for their impending revolt, readily found some in the legends of History. The result, as you know, was the storming of the Bastille, but instead of finding scores and more of wretched victims of despotism, the liberators found exactly seven inmates—hardly the hordes History suggests. Nor was any of the seven of any importance in the game then afoot, the French Revolution. Their names were Solages, Whyte, Tavernier, Béchade, La Corrège, Pujade, and Laroche. Count Solages was not exactly languishing in durance vile but was a loony put away by his family. After he was released he went to the Hôtel Rouen, where his board and room were paid for by the District of Oratoire. Whyte, giving Charles Dickens his inspiration for *A Tale of Two Cities,* had a long white beard when released and was a striking figure in the liberation parade, proving beyond all historical doubt that the Bastille was a wicked thing. After the parade Whyte returned to his lunacy and was put into an asylum at Charenton. Four of the seven were by no means political victims but had been convicted of forgery in a proper court of law and were merely serving their sentences. They disappeared during the excitement. Thus it was, and the "storming" of the Bastille served to arouse *les enfants de la patrie* (if you will excuse my French) to their duty to the common weal. A park now occupies the square where the Bastille once stood. A broken-down printing press, found in the rubble of the Bastille dungeon, was exhibited to the French People as an instrument of torture, which is no doubt as close as History can come to the Truth of the Fourteenth of July.

In conclusion, may I express my gratitude to the several foundations that made this study possible, and to Mrs. Thelma W. Peterson, who permitted me to park in her driveway on afternoons when I consulted the Free Public Library. I thank you. [Prolonged applause.]

The annual infusion of suchlike erudition had its effect, and Bill and I have never been unproud of our contributions to the uplift of the northern townships. We realized immediately that to sustain such high quality would be a challenge, but we feel that to some extent we have succeeded, and the Great Maine Woods are consequently indebted to us for much that is sapient and gracious. Our annual Bastille Day observances, alone, are notable. Bill is in complete charge, and his menu begins with French toast for breakfast, accompanied by our rendering "La Marseillaise" (whistled in French) and a relaxing day spent in meditating about liberty, equality, and fraternity. The evening banquet consists of knackwurst, sauerkraut, pumpernickel, imported St. Pauli Girl beer, and the *Echtedeutscheheitkartoffelsalat* for which he is justifiably famous. On the most previous occasion he delivered a eulogy on Dr. Joseph Ignace Guillotin, who invented the guillotine and made the French Revolution possible. I then read a few selections from the love letters of Mme. Defarge.

One year we engaged the girl motorcycle zouaves of the Misses Proctor School of the Ballet, of Monson, who reenacted the Battle of Ratisbon in five acts. So now when we return from our Grandfathers' Retreats, we are able to tell our inquiring friends just what we do up there in that vast wilderness. We don't do nothin'.

THE CARIBOU CLUB

It's got just about everything in it except whisky.
    —*Pierre Benoit, at Boundary Motel*

When Felix Fernald had his first date with Velma, he brought
her home at a decent hour, and when she went in the house,
her parents wanted to know what her new boyfriend was
like. Velma said, "Well, he looks just like a bull moose."
Velma's description was often corroborated by Felix himself,
who had no illusions about his physog, and he used to say,
"I'm the homeliest man that ever worked for Great Northern
Paper." He was always pleased that nobody challenged his
title. Felix, in our time, was the veteran woods clerk for
Northern and was based at Pittston Farm, past which Bill
and I took the Rainey Brook road up to our Baker Lake tent
site.

The word "farm" has special meaning up in that country.
It is a base, a depot, a headquarters for the company forest
operation. In the beginning it was labeled a farm because it
grew hay for the horses, and in the summer the horses were
kept there until snow came again and tree harvesting
resumed. Grant's Farm, Michaud Farm, Pittston Farm—Pittston Farm was so called because it was on the original Pittston Academy Grant, at the confluence of the North and
South branches of the Penobscot River, just upstream from
Seboomook Lake. The farm had a considerable complex of
buildings: offices for Felix and friends, machine shops, sta-

bles and garages, a telephone switchboard under command
of Velma, now Mrs. Fernald, and what amounted to a
hotel—bunkhouse, cookshack, and apartments for those
who lived at the farm. Mr. and Mrs. Lionel Long of Clair,
New Brunswick, were hostess and cook—she a charming
madame of dark beauty and Lionel the beanhole bean and
angel cake champion of all the Maine Woods.

The telephone switchboard closed around suppertime, so
it was imprudent to have any dire emergencies after Velma
pulled her plug. But in duty hours she had her finger on the
pulse of everything beyond Mount Kineo and this side of the
Last Hooraw. She knew where everybody was, or should be.
The single-wire forest telephone lines crackled and hummed,
but game wardens, forestry rangers, company workers could
crank the old magneto and find Velma ready for any emergency, or just to chitchat and brighten a gloom day in a
boomhouse.

So the first day Bill and I were in camp at Baker Lake, we
had sorted things out and set things right, and in the beauty
of the evening we were watching a moose dip for lily stems
and enjoying our wee schnaps. It was the morning and the
evening and we could see that it was good. We had a campfire dwindling to cooking embers, with steak and potatoes
standing by, and the gurgle of running water where the St.
John River first kicks up its heels made sweet concord in a
broad, wide world in which everything was the very best
possible. Bill and I were doing just what we came there to
do—getting acquainted. Now we heard an automobile, and
it swung off the International Paper road into the campsite
where we had been alone. It came beside our tent and
stopped. Then the most beautiful woman in the adjacent
three million acres stepped from the rider's side, and the most
god-awful ogre set the brake and alighted from the driver's
seat. Felix and Velma had come to call.

Since the North Maine Woods are so far from the solar
system, Bill and I were prepared to find a dearth of academic
opportunities and supposed that social pleasures would also

be few and far between. That is not true. If you have a four-
teen-room house and keep servants, you are in a way to
entertain, but if you want the extreme joy of pleasant company, be in a tent at Baker Lake. No, Felix and Velma had
taken supper before leaving Pittston Farm and had come
along just to see that we were making out, but they might
have a touch of cordial to soothe the dust of a July woods
road. They stayed well after Bill and I had eaten and the sun
had gone down, and drove back to Pittston Farm, mission
accomplished. Bill and I turned in, satisfied with everything.
Felix had invited us to go to Ste.-Aurélie the next afternoon
to assemble at Boundary Motel with certain Great Northern
Paper Company people who were having a retirement party
"for one of the Bessey boys." The whole Bessey family had
been important people for the company, and sending one of
'em off to retirement made a most special occasion.

Ste.-Aurélie, Bill and I found out, has been something of
a frolic spot over the years for Great Northern folks isolated
in that direction. It is a border town, entirely French, but not
exactly a point of entry. The gate between Maine and Quebec is attended daytimes by United States and Canadian customs officers, but a passport from either country doesn't
necessarily let you pass. The boundary is the western end of
the International Paper Company road, and unless you have
a pass from that company, you don't pass. All the Canadians
who come that way to work in the Maine Woods have such
passes, and are known anyway. Bill and I had such a pass,
temporary, and so arrived at the gate and went into Canada.
We told the Canadian officer that we wanted to tank up with
gasoline, and we had been invited to a soiree at Boundary
Motel. He smiled like a sunrise and said, *"Soyez prudent!"*

Directly beyond the boundary gate there was a convenience store with a BP pump, and beside it the Canadian customs office. Next was Boundary Motel, which seemed more
than ample for a community like Ste.-Aurélie. Besides what
has been mentioned, the rest of the community was the Red
Mill, a hundred yards up the road, which advertised beer on

draft and *danseuses*. Bill and I were told there is a theatrical agency in Montreal that supplies young ladies who disrobe and dance to jukebox music. There's a new girl every week, but the spectators (we were told!) are rather much the same old beer drinkers.

When Bill and I entered Boundary Motel, we were greeted by the proprietor, Benoit Caron, whose wife was chambermaid and cook, and their son, Pierre, who was the dining-room waiter and the bartender and who was wearing a tuxedo. He was then fourteen years of age. Benoit and his wife lacked English, but Pierre told us to put our vehicle on the Maine side of the gate if we planned to go back to Baker Lake that night.

Baker Lake?

Yes, Felix Fernald had telephoned from Pittston Farm and told them to give Bill and me good care.

Bill said, "I've been told some of the Canadian ales are rather good. I think a beer would ease that road dust." But when Pierre brought our glasses, they were of the champagne style, and the contents were not Labatt or O'Keefe or Molson, or even le Dow. "What's this?" I asked Pierre.

"Caribou—Felix Fernald!"

Thus Bill and I became members of the infamous Caribou Club, attainable only at Boundary Motel by taking a drink called a Caribou, which is available only at that place and is composed of secret ingredients known only to the family of Benoit Caron.

As well as the senior clerk at Pittston Farm, Felix became a company historian, and his weekly issues of the *Pittston Farm News* record many a fact. You'll find a file of that mimeographed publication in the Lumberman's Museum at Patten, Maine. In his issue of June 13, 1966, he wrote:

It was just 33 years ago today that we'uns drove into North Twin Dam to begin our career with GNP Company. It was sure some shock to be rolled out of bed at four o'clock in the morning to eat a hurried breakfast

then enjoy the sunrise while hiking to the head of Qua-
kish Lake to spend the balance of the daylight hours
pushing pulpwood to and fro. First lunch was at 9:00
o'clock at which time Joe Hachey, cookee, would show
up with a pail of baked beans and a bucket of biscuits.
At 2:30 Joe would show up again with the second lunch,
which was also beans and biscuits. At eight o'clock we
would be plodding our way back to the boom house
and by the time we sat down for our evening repast it
was necessary to light the kerosene lamps.

So Felix was the proper hand to arrange a farewell party
for a fellow veteran, and Bill and I sat with about a hundred
Great Northern folks, all members of the Caribou Club, and
we had just as fine a time as anybody else. When it came
time for the eulogy to "one of the Besseys," Felix rapped for
attention, positioned a microphone, took out his teeth, and
laid them on the piano top, where they smiled pleasantly at
the assembly all during the harangue. Then Felix spoke for
thirty minutes about the sterling qualities of the guest of
honor, who, through thick and thin, in prosperity and adver-
sity, fair weather and foul, had faithfully performed his
duties and much more in a full lifetime of loyalty to the company—a loyalty that would endear him forever to his fellow
workers who were now gathered to share his happiness and
wish him well.

But nobody heard a word Felix said, since the microphone
had not been plugged into an outlet of the Quebec Hydro-
electric System. Nobody, understandably, was about to call
attention to this oversight. During Felix's stirring remarks
the guest of honor went to the men's room.

We heard later that Del Bates, clerk at the Scott Brook
Lumber Camp operation, decided that because of the lateness
of the hour, he would not attempt to drive back to Maine and
so took a room in the motel. During the night Del became
confused, somehow, and made use of the big tub in the corri-
dor otherwise reserved for the motel's aspidistra. Benoit

Caron spoke to Del with some heat about this and ordered Del never to darken his door again. But (we were told) since Del didn't understand a word of French, no great harm was done.

Another consequence of that memorable occasion came a year later, when Bill was mentioned in the *Pittston Farm News*. Felix had been impressed with the idea of Bill's illustrated lecture about Washington's generals. So he announced that the next meeting of the Caribou Club would present Professor Downbirch with his celebrated historical lecture about General Washington's privates.

WELCOME, GENTLEMEN!

> A man of dry wit and shrewdness, and a general intelligence I had not looked for in the backwoods. In fact, the deeper you penetrate into the woods, the more intelligent, and, in one sense, the less countrified do you find the inhabitants. . . .
> —*Thoreau, at the mouth of Little Schoodic, concerning "Uncle George" McCauslin*

Membership in the very esoteric Caribou Club not only was a warm experience for the first introduction to our Maine Woods but turned out to be a tremendous, if vague, asset to enrich the following three decades of our annual Grandfathers' Retreats. The morning after, still a-tingle from the Bessey Farewell, Bill and I set the camp to rights, strung our fly rods, and gave a whirl at two-three likely-looking trout brooks in the vicinity. I had explained to Bill, the tenderfoot, that the prospects of a bulging creel were slim, and then I added that honest trout hunters speak of creels but use a gad. A gad is a forked limb of an alder on which breakfast trout are to be gilled for transport to the fire. A creel is a basket available at L. L. Bean and used in classy angling advertisements in the Abercrombie & Fitch catalog. Well, it was mid-July and the blackflies had pretty well waned, the water was low in the streams, and the early birds from both Canada and the United States had long since tromped their paths from pool to pool downstream and back. It would be the odd one if we got one. And we didn't get one, in spite of my having explained to Bill that I could find 'em when others couldn't, and for tomorrow's breakfast he would have trout.

I suggested we go back by Rainey Brook that afternoon and see if the South Branch would produce. The South Branch would have more water, and not far below Canada Falls there were a couple of excellent pools before the stream went into a long cascade of white water—which was great fun to fish and gave a challenge if one struck. On the way we passed Pittston Farm, and we swung in to thank Felix Fernald for his hospitality and entertainment of the previous evening at Boundary Motel. Felix was talking company business in his office with Leo Thibodeau.

Leo was employment manager for Great Northern, and while he did his work in a country well peopled with French-Canadians, Leo was a natural-born citizen of the United States, an Acadian from the St. John Valley, a descendant of the Nova Scotia *colons* who had been dispersed in the great Evangeline disruption of 1755. The minute Leo opened his head, and he was perfectly at home in both English and French, you knew that he was different from the choppers brought in from Quebec. He had a rolling accent, and it showed "the Valley" equally in either tongue. He was rollicking good-humored, and congratulated Bill and me on being initiated, and feigned to offer the grip and word as a fellow traveler along the right road. We said we were on our way to try the South Branch, as the Baker Lake scenery seemed lacking in trouts.

Leo said, "You might get a strike, but it's July and late. Tell you what—you go try the rips and be back here at noon and after dinner I'll fix you up with some panfish."

So we had "dinner" with Leo and the Great Northern folks at Pittston Farm, and we met Lionel and Mrs. Long and had a piece of her sugar pie as well as very fine beefsteaks and with-its. In those days when Great Northern was feeding its crews, the company's commissary had a decided clout in the wholesale market, and when Lionel Long specified steaks,

everybody knew what he meant. And Leo was high enough
in the company roster so Lionel didn't stint. Leo handed us a
note and said, "Give this to Adelard Gilbert [zhil-bare] at
Scott Brook Camp." So that same day we got acquainted
with the fabulous pulpwood King, Adelard, and his camp
clerk, the equally fabulous and perhaps incredible Delmont
Bates. At least Adelard was believable.

True to Maine Woods custom, before Leo finished his
business with Felix and left Pittston Farm, he cranked Del
Bates on the woods telephone to alert him that Bill and I
were on the way. Scott Brook Camp (now completely
removed and the clearing regrown) at that time had about
150 men, including scalers, truck drivers, teamsters, machin-
ists, and so on, and the position of clerk in a camp of that size
was by no means a small job. So Del knew we were on our
way. Over the years, access to the Scott Brook Camp
changed as new roads were built and old ones washed away.
We arrived from Seboomook Dam and the Beanpot Mountain road, and as we drove up an incline to get our first sight
of a building, we saw a huge Jolly Roger on a staff over the
clerk's office—the cock shop, so called. It was Del's *signum
auctoritatis*. Made from a bedsheet and therefore bedsheet size,
the skull and crossbones were a ludicrous ornamentation for
the otherwise efficient layout of Scott Brook Camp. As we
pulled up under the flag, we were positioned for a panorama
view of the complex. Beside the cock shop stood a modern
house trailer (for the camp boss, Adelard Gilbert) and good
tight camps in rows for the men. The cookshack was sizable,
and between it and the cock shop were two twenty-thousand-gallon fuel tanks—gasoline and diesel. The bathhouse
was beyond, supported by a generator shed with its gasoline
engine that ran day and night; we could hear it the instant we
killed the ignition. There were work sheds of one kind and
another, and just beyond the whole complex was a sawmill
with stacked lumber. Great Northern used boards and timber
enough to keep this mill busy just for company purposes.

But by now our presence was known, and from the cock

shop screen door burst a man who was built a good deal like
a hubbard squash, and he came rolling down the steps to
greet us with "Gentlemen! Gentlemen, welcome to Scott
Brook!" The moment is memorable and will linger with Bill
and me forever. Delmont Bates remains unequaled among
the gracious, kind, hospitable, friendly, worth-knowing
Great Northern folks of our Maine Woods experience. He
always called us gentlemen. A top Great Northern man told
us one July, "If I was told to set up a new lumber camp and
could have my choice of clerks, I'd ask for Del Bates."

Having heard from Leo (and Velma) that Bill and I were
on the way, Clerk Bates knew our errand, and shortly he
said, "Adelard will be right along; he went to the woods."
His pickup truck wheeled into camp shortly, and as the dust
settled, we saw Adelard step down and come towards us, his
hands at his sides but the palms turned backwards, a manner
of walking we found was peculiar to Adelard so anybody
could tell him a mile away. At the moment he was top contractor for Great Northern, and all the other contractors
wondered how Adelard got so many more cords than they
did. Adelard's Engish was meager, so we bonjoured and I
gave him Leo's note. Adelard looked at it, said "Bime-by,"
and handed the note back to me. It was in French: "Dear
Adelard, please do me the favor of showing John and Bill
where to find some trouts, Leo."

"Bime-by" simply meant in the late afternoon, when the
trout, after a bright day, would begin to feed. Meantime, Bill
and I visited with Del Bates in his cock shop and got some
insight into the duties of a clerk. He still had his landline
telephone, although a few summers later Great Northern
turned to radio. He had a typewriter but was still doing a
good part of his bookkeeping in great ledgers; he paused a
moment to make an entry that two visitors had just arrived.
Behind his desk he had the shelves of stock that were "the
company store." In earlier days this amounted to quite an
inventory as choppers came in the fall and stayed all winter.
But now the men went back to Canada for weekends *(week-*

end is a perfectly good Maine Woods French word—*le week-end*) and could bring things back from Canadian stores. Del still offered razor blades, candy bars, and work gloves, as well as spray cans of insect death, but the days when the wangan (or company) store was truly important had passed. Del was also first-aid man for the camp, and a sign on the cookshack porch attested that while this was important, it wasn't too demanding; the sign said the camp had 141 days without a lost-time accident. But Del did his desk work in constant dread that a chain saw could lash out and interrupt him. He showed us a Prentiss & Carlisle map of the region, tacked to the wall, and traced the road from Scott Brook over to Caucomagomac Lake, a matter of ten miles. "Next time you come," he said, "don't bother with a damn tent. I've got the key to the company camp at Cauc Dam, and it'll be ready for you." So our tenting in the Maine Woods amounted to that first Retreat, and the next July Del gave us the key to sumptuous living.

It was about four o'clock when Adelard again came from the woods, dust storm and all, and motioned us into his pickup. Riding with Adelard (or with any experienced North Woods driver) is an occasion for prayer, and Bill and I were grateful when Adelard came to the wooden bridge over Withee Brook and pulled to a stop among the raspberry bushes. He led us a few rods down the brook, through breast-high puckerbrush, and then motioned us onto a plank that was suspended over the water on short posts—a contrivance Mainers call a staddle. From the staddle we had casting room downstream, right to a mare's nest of twigs and branches formed as sticks and limbs had been brought down by the current. Adelard pointed and said, *"Met' l'mouche là."* In six casts I took six ten-inch trout, and then Adelard drove us frantically from his own private angling preserve back to Scott Brook Lumber Camp, which Bill and I were to visit again and again with eager anticipation. We outlasted the place. Del and Adelard retired at about the same time, and then the camp became obsolete. Logs were now being harvested in another way. The buildings were moved to other places, the area bulldozed clear, and new trees were beginning a new cycle. Del, in memory, continues to prove the Thoreauvian hypothesis that distance into the Maine Woods makes less countrified inhabitants. And when Adelard retired, he took his *bonne femme* to France on an extended holiday to visit the Normandy village from which their *aïeux* had come to Canadaw so many years ago. He asked slyly on his postcard from Caen if Withee Brook still had trouts. It does, but the "staddle" washed away the next freshet after Adelard retired.

LIGHTNING STRIKES

I doubt if men ever made a trade of heroism.
— *Thoreau, as he thought of Achilles in
terms of lumber camp derring-do*

On his first canoe trip north of Moosehead Lake with Joe Polis,
his Penobscot Indian guide, Thoreau was much taken with
the simple Amerind, and clearly this began his interest in the
subject, which was to continue the rest of his life. He keeps
asking Joe to show him various lores, to give the Indian
names of places and things, and to tell what those names
mean. He reveals that he has already studied Father Rasle's
Indian dictionary, and he has told us that Indians seemingly
dislike to climb mountains—which he attributes to supersti-
tion. Thoreau certainly begins to compare the unenlightened
savage with civilized man and offers considerable evidence
that this difference is daily on his mind. There is accordingly
a chuckle when Joe Polis says that he had never climbed
Kineo Mountain, which is then most evident on the skyline
ahead, but adds that he has been to Boston, New York, Philadelphia, and Washington. He tells Thoreau that in Boston
he called on Daniel Webster and was cordially received.
Moreover, he had been to the Maine Statehouse in Augusta
as the tribal representative for the Penobscot Nation, and had
gone afterwards to an intertribal powwow that brought
together the storied chieftains of the American Indians right
through to the Pacific coast.

Thoreau seems not to have found this amusing, but Bill
and I were delighted to learn from Clerk Delmont Bates of
the Scott Brook Lumber Camp of the Great Northern Paper
Company that he had recently been given a leave of absence
so he could perform his duties in the Maine legislature as
the elected representative (Republican) of his native town of
Patten. He explained to Bill and me that he got elected
because he was the only man in town who owned a suit of
clothes.

On an early retreat Bill and I noticed that by Del's office
chair he kept an unabridged dictionary of the English language, and on a stand close by was a pile of crossword puzzle
books, such as abound in certain stores. And it has always
been the Law of the Land that anybody going into the woods
pause en route to pick up a supply of reading matter—newspapers, magazines, joke books, and whatever else will while
away the tedium of a wet day in camp. Bill and I stopped in
Newport to stock up for Del, and besides newspapers and
magazines we had twenty or twenty-five crossword puzzle
books. When we gave the bundle to Del, he thumbed
through them, and he said, "Done this one, done this one,
done that one. Ah! Haven't seen this one." Had we paid better attention to Del's conversations, we'd have known that
his vocabulary had been acquired somewhere. Del had several brothers, and they all got through Patten High School.
Del's father was a "walking boss" in the Maine forests about
Patten, which at that time was a busy-busy long log area. A
walking boss had several chopping camps to oversee and
would "walk" from one to the other, passing a night here
and going on to another camp in the morning. Del told us
his father shrewdly divided his work so he was always home
for the weekend. And he said it was a house rule that which-
ever boy got in last on Saturday night was always the one to
get up at daybreak and milk the family cow. Del said he
never knew how his father kept informed as to which of his
sons was last-one-in, but he always did. Del felt this small
house rule had something to do with the conduct of family

affairs and the upright quality of the boys' moral attitudes. Of the boys, Del was selected by his father as the one most likely to make a good lumber camp clerk, so after finishing high school, Del was off to Boston to study accounting and bookkeeping.

Del told Bill and me that his father would take him into the woods now and then to introduce him to lumber camp ways, and he always found that fun; instead of walking from camp to camp, his father traveled by sleigh—a high-stepping mare and a sturdy set-over sleigh pung. At one camp there chanced to be but one bunk unoccupied, and Del and his father shared it. Del, still a boy eager to please his father, began dreaming about this precept and that admonishment, and he twisted and turned in his sleep until his father kicked him out of bed. Del told us not one word came from his father, and the rest of that night on a chair was the longest he ever spent. Once in the pung and on the way, his father said, "Del, always leave your work on your desk; a good night's sleep depends on it."

Although Bill and I were in and out of the Scott Brook Camp during our Retreats, we never spent a night there. One July we were tucked nicely in our dam tender's camp ten miles away, and there came up a jerooshly great thunder-shower that played around the lakes and mountains for well over a noisy hour. Some of the strikes were close enough to our camp so we heard the snaps and smelled the brimstone. But over at the Scott Brook Lumber Camp Old Zeus took better aim, and one of his best efforts clipped the twenty-thousand-gallon gasoline tank that stood (along with a diesel fuel tank) right outside the cock shop wall where Delmont Bates was sound asleep, having left his work on his desk. Since it was an extremely hot night (ideal for the finest thunder bumpers), Del was not wearing a sleeping garment and he was using no bedcover.

When the bolt of lightning hit the gasoline tank, it brought every man in camp, including Mr. Bates, to attention, but it did not cause an explosion. The only sound was that of the thunder, which should not be lightly dismissed. But that was enough to bring the boys out, so every chopper was standing in awe to see Mr. Bates emerge from his camp, exhibit his tail generously, and disappear down the road to Beanpot Mountain in determined haste. The spectacle was easily watched, because the lightning had set afire the vapors from a venthole on the top of the tank, and like a giant blowtorch, a stream of flame was shooting three hundred feet into the sky and there was no darkness whatever in miles around.

Adelard Gilbert, boss, kept his cool and called for a ladder and a wet blanket, which were readily brought, and he tossed the blanket over the blowhole and darkness was restored. They told Bill and me that Del Bates appeared back at his cock shop in the middle of the forenoon just in time to begin the week's payroll. It was his blanket, hanging idly over his porch railing, that Adelard had carried up the ladder. Del sometimes would quote Henry David Thoreau. This time he said, "It is characteristic of wisdom not to do desperate things."

On several Retreats Bill and I broke camp and started home on a Sunday, and Del would invite us to stop and have breakfast with him before we "lit out down the trail for town." These were momentous breakfasts. The crew had all gone out to Canadian homes for the weekend, leaving only Del and the hostler in camp. Although machinery was moving in, Scott Brook still used a half dozen teams. Romeo Bolduc was the hostler, but I always called him M'sieu Chevalier. Del, who resisted French even though in a position to learn it, never knew why that was funny, but M. Chevalier chuckled over it. On weekends M. Chevalier became the camp cook, and he and Del kept Bachelors Hall. M. Chevalier loved to cook and was good at it. He had refrigerator, freezer, and stock shelves to work from—the same supplies the regular cooks used to feed 150 men. By the time Bill and I were packed and ready to start out, M. Chevalier had everything ready and Del would be on the porch waiting for our arrival. When he saw us coming around the bend, he would jump and pound the come-and-get-it—the dinner gong—in a ceremonial manner that could be heard for ten miles except some psychologist decided that ten miles away there's no noise if there's nobody there to hear it. M. Chevalier would dish up forty-dollar breakfasts for the four of us and keep his lavish desserts in the steam table until we'd finished the pork chops and the potatoes and all the other things. And Del would regale us with his yarns.

BILL'S FIRST SALMON

We had been told that we should here find trout enough;
so while some prepared the camp the rest fell to fishing.
—*Thoreau at the mouth of Abol Stream*
on his way to Ktaadn

There seems to be no internal evidence that Thoreau tried for or
caught a Maine salmon, and I believe that had he done so he
would never have remained silent about it. Piscator says in
a certain treatise on angling that the salmon is the king of
freshwater fishes, and Bill and I are willing to concede that.
Our Maine salmon must never be mistaken for anything
found on the Pacific side; ours is either the Atlantic salmon,
Salmo salar, which is a sea-run variety, or the *Salmo sebago,*
which is a landlocked version of what, before the Ice Age,
was the same thing. The Atlantic salmon can be caught today
only in Maine and in the streams of Atlantic Canada. Our
landlocked kind is found in Maine and New Hampshire and
in Canada, where it is termed a ouananiche. It is simply a sea-
run salmon that was once entrapped while upstream about
replenishing and was unable to get back to salt water. You
are not likely to find an eastern salmon in a tin can.

Thoreau was not a purist and used salt pork to hook his
first trout. Then he cut pieces off that trout to hook more.
He was, accordingly, unsuited by instinct to fish for the finest kind. Bill and I, true to angling gentility, have done all
our fishing with artificial lures, and when for any reason we

return unrewarded to camp, that's what we have hot dogs for. It was a glorious afternoon on a glorious Retreat that Bill took his first salmon out of Loon Lake Stream. I knew that Bill had fished at Kennebago Lake before our Grandfathers' Retreats began, and because Kennebago is fine salmon water, I just supposed he was an old hand at the King of Fishes. I was wrong; trout, yes, but not yet a salmon. The waters of the West Branch would confer that honor upon him, and I was going to be privileged to watch.

When an angler presents his lure correctly to a salmon, and His Piscatorial Majesty deigns to approach, the coming together, as with some varieties of fish, is not a nibble. A nibble is sometimes the word, but with a salmon it is more like the Cannonball Express running into a pier of the G. Washington Bridge. A salmon means to get it. The word is "strike." When a salmon strikes your lure and realizes he has been swindled, you have exactly one ten-millionth of a second before he comes out of the water and goes into the sky with a vast shudder that is intended to free that fly and leave it up there in the air to fend for itself—and usually does. The alert and experienced angler knows how to frustrate this effort, but the novice or the inattentive most often concludes this encounter right there with a slack line and talking to himself. If, however, the salmon returns to the same hole in the water from which he came with everything still attached, it means the angler is in for quite some minutes of superior entertainment. A salmon will make several of these desperate leaps and between them will make "runs." He swims this way or that way or all points of the compass at once, testing the angler's skill and often finding it lacking. A prudent angler will not dispute with a salmon at this time but will let him make his leaps and his runs as he pleases, being only careful to keep the line reasonably taut. You let a salmon have a suggestion of a slack line while he is engaged in these exercises, and you'll have only to brag about the big one that got away.

So Bill and I came to see how things were at Loon Lake

Stream, and as there was no fishway in the Loon Lake Dam at that time, we could tackle the pools just below. (Since then a new dam was built with a concrete fish ladder, and anglers must keep 150 feet away—conservation rule. It's not cricket to interrupt a salmon who is concentrating at the moment on joining his lady friend at the other end of honeymoon lane.) Still not knowing that Bill had yet to take a salmon, I motioned him to the nigh side of the upper pool and then stood a moment to watch while he unlimbered his line and made a few casts.

Then I walked up the banking, crossed over the dam, and came down to the same pool but on the far side of the stream. Good view of each other, and distance enough so we wouldn't snag lines, but the rush of water prevented speaking. We went to fishing.

It is hard to explain the niceties of angling to a great many people who ask. Isaak Walton called fishing "the contemplative man's recreation," and that's a good place to start. With fly fishing, there is a rhythmic symphony of casting and retrieving which occupies the hands and the eyes, but it becomes second nature and the angler pays little attention to it. Now and then inattention causes a hook to tangle in an alder behind you, and the reverie of casting is interrupted while you get your fly back, and sometimes this makes a good time to change flies. Until you find something that King Salmon will presume tasty, you try this one and that one. Mostly you just keep on casting and retrieving and fade into a happy haze of pleasant inconsequence—a world completely unworldly with just You and God and the chance of a Salmon. All the birds sing for you. The muskrat and the mink disport for you, and the bullfrog is ready to sit there and stare for days and days and days. The sky is bright, and no doubt too bright for fishing, but what of that? Think of the millions and millions of people in this world who have no idea where you are! Lo! There comes a moose to wade and feast. And there's a bald eagle making great circles. Lift thine eyes now and then, and maybe the mate will appear.

But don't drift off into indifference because King Salmon is noted for attacking when his enemy is unwary.

As for me, on the far side of Bill's pool, I was watching the bull moose downstream and I had seen the eagle and the mink, and I was casting and retrieving, and I was also ready if a salmon decided to surprise me. For that matter, I was also keeping an eye on Bill's line—mostly so I'd be ready to pull in my line and leave the pool to him if he had a strike.

He had a strike.

It was a good, clean strike—the kind a salmon makes when he wants to show off. Bill's fly, cast a little upstream, had drifted with the current to the end of his line length, making its little pop-up on the surface. The salmon actually took the fly at that instant when direction changed, which meant the fish set the hook himself by his own touch. Bill, however, was ready, and his slack line was in his left hand when the salmon rose into the eagle's sky and shook water over an acre and a half. As the salmon went down, I could see that Bill was in control, and I was satisfied he would do everything right. I took in my line and laid my fly rod against some bushes. I had the best seat in the house, and I sat down.

Bill was "on" that salmon so the hand was just coming up to forty-six golden minutes. The fish made six leaps before he was convinced, and his runs took him in and out of quick water so Bill needed utmost judgment with each run. Reclining on that opposite banking, I admired Bill's finesse and joyed along with him at every movement of his rod.

Now the damnedest thing happened.

As Bill stood there at the edge of the water, a duck came from the bushes behind him and passed between his legs into the drink! Please permit me to do a Thoreau with this one! She was a female *Mergus merganrer americanus,* our commonest inland waterfowl, and she had just brought her brood over Loon Lake Dam to herd the ducklings into the stream below. She did not know that Bill was anywhere about. When she became aware of Bill, she let out an ungodly squawk which assembled her family, and immediately her brood boiled out between Bill's legs, hit the water, and Momma and all were off down Loon Lake Stream at an estimated 85 mph. Bill paid no attention, and after about ten minutes more he had his salmon ashore. The show was over. I picked up my rod and tackle box, recrossed the dam, and came to admire the salmon and congratulate its owner.

Bill was standing over the beautiful fish, and I must say a suspicion of disbelief hovered about his vicinity. Was there an effort to appear nonchalant?

Bill said, "My first salmon!" It was only then I knew.

"You did everything precisely right!" I said.

Bill said, "I wasn't about to lose that one!"

"Did you see that damn sheldrake?" I asked.

Bill said, "Wasn't that something to see? She had thirteen little ones."

And he was right. She had thirteen, but to Bill and me there seemed nothing unlucky about that.

SOME BETTER YEARS

Feigning royal interest when he had little, King Charles asked what the Pilgrims might do in the American wilderness to sustain themselves, and was told they expected to fish. His Majesty said, "Well, it was the Apostles' own calling."

In our thirty visits to Thoreau's broad Maine Woods, Bill and I were not often thwarted to the extent that trout or salmon disappeared from our joys. Some years we worked hard and found few fish. There were years a little hard work paid off. There were also years when we did well and threw back so many we never told about it; it's a way of fishing too many people refuse to believe. Many a year we were skunked until we trudged through swampy places to find a beaver flowage that nobody else had seduced. The year Bill got his first salmon at Loon Lake Stream we felt that one trophy made our summer, and we didn't fish the rest of our week.

Another summer we took a canoe. I had a twenty-foot guide's model, canvas, and I made a rack to carry it on the pickup. We took it along for the express purpose of fishing the Scott Brook Deadwater. Scott Brook is a tributary to Loon Stream, the same place where Bill counted the merganser ducks, and the deadwater is up near the source. I think it may be physically impossible to walk out enough to fish the deadwater from shore because of swampy land and head-high bushes. Bill and I were told we could put a canoe in by carrying it a short distance and then paddling the quiet water for about two miles. Folks who knew the deadwater said it was fantastically erratic. You could work your tail off getting in there and find you had come on a day when the trout refused to play. Oh, the trout were there, all right, but they'd sulk, or observe some special holiday. If you don't get a rise in five minutes, they told us, quit and come out. We found this was true. We packed refreshments, gaffled my canoe and pushed it through ten feet of hackleberry bushes to the water, climbed in, and like a yellow leaf in autumn, like a yellow water lily, we silently reached the far end, and we were where they told us to fish—the spot where we could first hear in the distance the diesel engine that drives the AC generator for Scott Brook Lumber Camp. We knew it was the place, because as we glided to a stop and unlimbered our killick, trout were jumping all over the place—some within inches of our gunnels. That was one of our best afternoons.

Bill took the first trout and in ceremonial custom kept it. That is to propitiate the Great Spirit Ishywhoops, who long ago sent down word that if you don't keep the first one, you won't catch another. After that we began matching them for size and threw back anything less than eleven inches and more than twelve inches. We kept twenty-three such trout, and we had been fishing all of fifteen minutes. The number twenty-three takes into account the first one, which was small, and the fact that the daily limit on Scott Brook is one dozen to a person. That was the open law for that county at that time; it has since been much reduced. And the number takes into account that Bill and I were planning to entertain the following night with the ineffable delicacy of a woodsman's trout chowder, commenced right after morning prayers and allowed to osmosify leisurely until the late afternoon, when the guests arrive in eager fettle.

On the way out we were interrupted. We were yanking our canoe through the puckerbrush to tie it on the pickup truck for the ride back to camp, and directly in our way on the end of a blowdown we found a handsome and well-turned-out State of Maine game warden whittling at a stick,

and he said, "Hello, boys!" with a jolly manner that indicated
he expected to see us in a day or so down at the County
Courthouse in Dover-Foxcroft, where Stickler Judge Grab-
All likes to throw his book at trout poachers.

"Hello yourself," I reciprocated. "Been waiting long?"

"Couple of hours, maybe not quite."

"Malcolm?" I asked.

"Eyah, Malcolm. You know Malcolm?"

"Better'n that—Malcolm knows us."

The way they work that—Malcolm Mayheu, who is the
flying game warden out of Greenville (or was; he's now
retired), keeps watch of the ponds that pass beneath him, and
when he sees a boat or canoe, he radios and a ground warden
gets the alert. Works all right, and every year they nail
enough innocent poachers to pay the wardens princely
wages. So this young man had been waiting at the only place
on the deadwater that we could take out our canoe.

No doubt he was disappointed that Bill and I were legal,
but at once he began to remark on our catch. "That's the best
string of trout I've seen this season!" he said. "What'll you
do with them?"

A reasonable question since we were so far in the woods
and he didn't know we had a gas refrigerator at our Great
Northern camp.

Bill said, "We contemplate a ceremonial trout chowder
tomorrow evening in the anterior nave of the vaulted ashmo-
lean adjacent to Bates Hall on the extensive campus of the
Caucomagomac Dam Institute of Fine and Coarse Art. We
should be honored to have you join us at six."

The warden stood up and said, "What was that you just
said?"

Bill told him to come for supper, that we were having
some friends in for chowder.

That was a momentous feast. A trout chowder follows the
general rule for a Yankee audience. But preparing the trout
meat takes a little time. The trout are dressed, and heads and
tails donated to the wildlife of the region. Then the little dar-

lings are wrapped in a clean dishcloth, making a suitable sack, and are hung in the steam from a proper kettle until the meat is cooked sufficiently so the bones and skin will come away readily. Pick away until you have the flesh clean; fingers do it best. Bill and I did this the following morning and set the whopping great dish of clear-quill trout meat into the Servel to bide. Meantime, we had started word along the sylvan corridors that we were entertaining, and not counting our game warden, we had fourteen ready acceptances. We were pleased to hear that Cora Bates had come over from Patten to weekend with Del and would grace the head of our otherwise masculine table.

Soon after our frugal noon repast, Bill and I began. Using the largest pot in the camp, we covered the bottom well with diced salt pork, and after debating if we had enough, we added some more. The heat was applied, and with a gentle flame the pork shortly responded and permeated the camp with the delightful aroma associated therewith, and Bill and I took turns reverently stirring so that we might garner the juice but not render the pork crispy. That comes later.

So we added all the onions we had in camp, sliced and diced, after removing the pork scraps and leaving just the fat, and we sang "Lloyd George Knows My Father" and "A Little Town in New Hampshire," and repeated the 37 Articles of Faith of the Newcomen Society, and then we took the water pails down to the pond and inspected the scenery before we brought them back full of water. Onions require careful treatment when indulging in pork fat osmosis. In due time we could see that we were making splendid progress, so we made ready the potatoes. Judging when to add the potatoes calls for keen analysis of "translucency." When the onions are rightly that way, dump 'em in! Your trout chowder is now beyond the point of no return.

Having no fresh milk that late in the week, Bill and I mixed some dry milk powder and indulged comically in the usual argument as to whether we should make Holstein, Jersey, Ayrshire, and should we homogenize it by passing it through a washcloth. Then, to make sure, we opened a large can of evaporated milk, a maneuver that must always be accompanied by the woodsman's apt doggerel: "Just punch two holes in the sonofabitch!"

I would estimate it was now about half past two, or going on three, so we were well on schedule, and we tipped the waiting trout meat in with the pork fat, onions, and potatoes, leaving things to get acquainted under a cover. So far, liquid involved is slight, so the heat has been low. We are now about to add the milk, and it is well to warm it first. If the milk curdles, it doesn't mean you have to throw everything away, but it doesn't look as if the cook cared. The milk having been added, your trout (or any fish) chowder is now ready to mull along on a somewhat hotter flame and achieve its perfection to the Glory of God and the joy of its beholders. I don't care what *Gourmet* magazine tells you, don't do it. I know full well this world has all kinds of people who know more than I do, but don't do it!

The pork scraps, tried out in the beginning, have been waiting for further attention and may now be put in a smaller frypan and heated again. Don't overdo them, but get them a wee bit crispy, and add them to the chowder a short spell before serving time. With fourteen guests and the game warden, Bill and I made seventeen, so the twenty-four trout pretty much made another miracle of the loaves and the fishes. The next time Bill and I put a canoe on the Scott Brook Deadwater we whipped the water to a froth and never rose a trout.

Another year Bill and I went back to Ste.-Aurélie—something neither expected to do. We had tasted a Caribou and we cared not for *danseuses* and we didn't jibe with retirement parties. But on this Retreat we fell into fishermen's luck on Cauc Stream. We'd sung the evening hymns, propitiated everything, had our bountiful refection, and were just finishing with the dishpan. A prominent sunset was distributed over the western sky, and Bill said, "Betcha this is the one evening this season to fish the river!" At this we took our rods off the pegs, formed an academic procession, and chanting, "Brekekekex, ko-ax, ko-ax!" we marched in stately sobriety from our hallowed halls of learning to the marge, which is but a short perambulation, and found the situation salubrious. We began to cast, Bill somewhat downstream from me, and nothing happened.

The crepuscular light was diminishing, and below the dam as we were we had no more of the gorgeous red glow over the western mountain. It was approaching that moment when our eyes wouldn't see the line after we cast it. I recall some whistlers entertained us. The whistler, a duck, makes a whistling sound with its wings in flight, and a family of them was active as night descended. When flying up or down a stream, a whistler stays just above the water, but if it encounters a person, a moose, or anything that suggests caution, it will rise abruptly ten, twenty, maybe thirty feet to fly over it and then descend just as abruptly to the water again and keep on going—whistle, whistle, whistle. Now, as we fished in the last vestige of daylight, these whistlers passed up and down and rose and fell as they encountered me and Bill. And instead of going up once to pass us both in one maneuver, they ascended, descended, ascended, and descended and repeated on the way back.

Just then a salmon struck my fly. "Strike!" I called to Bill, and he came upstream to stand beside me with the net ready. We needed a net; it was a fine salmon. I think he wasn't so sizable as Bill's trophy fish from Loon Lake Stream, but he'd do. Bill netted him, and when he removed the fly, he tossed it away in the air and said, "OK!" I flipped the line, not so much to fish again as to straighten it for cranking on my reel, and as Bill was admiring the salmon in the dim light, I was obliged to interrupt his studies with "Hey! I got another!" The two salmon, both males, were out of the same clutch—head to head and tail to tail—and we still had minimum light enough to dress them by the stream before we returned to camp. But only just—the whistlers had ceased to fly by the time we were done.

Which is why Bill and I went again to Ste. Aurélie. When we returned to camp after this pleasure, we found water on the floor and found our Servel gas refrigerator had declined into a malfunction. Our precious ceremonial ice cubes were melting. There is no mechanism, no motor, to one of those, and a malfunction isn't supposed to occur unless the gas flame goes out. The flame was burning. We lost all our food and learned a year later that a mud wasp had nested in a vent tube, thus stopping the cooling process. Before the next July the tube had been cleaned. But now Bill and I were on our way to Ste.-Aurélie, to find somebody willing to be kind to two beautiful twenty-four-inch landlocked salmon who would never last the night in our July-tempered camp.

We knew the international gate would be closed at that hour, and we knew the United States Customs Bureau had a sign on the front door that said so. So we went to the back door, and Al Lagasse, who was then the resident official, opened the door to say, "Sorry, but it's after hours!" Then I said, "Al, we know that, and we know it is unlawful to give, offer, or otherwise make available any gift, emolument, reward, bribe, or article of value to customs and immigration officers, so at this late hour and to bring things to a successful conclusion, may we speak to your wife?" Now Al looked closer and saw who was there.

Mrs. Lagasse accepted those handsome salmon with joy and alacrity, and Bill and I went back to Cauc Lake Dam. We looked at the Servel, but couldn't imagine what was wrong with it. We did turn off the flame.

It was fifteen years later that my wife and I came down from Sherbrooke, Quebec, into Maine by way of the boundary town of Coburn Gore; that's the historical Arnold Trail to Quebec City. We pulled up at customs, ready for the officer to come out and ask who we might be. He came out. He said, "Well, hello! You bringing my wife some more fish?" Bill and I didn't know Al had been transferred.

A WASTELAND BANQUET

We ate off a large log which some freshet had thrown
up. This time we had a dish of arbor-vitae, or cedar-tea,
which the lumberer sometimes uses when other herbs
fail.—

"A quart of arbor-vitae
To make him strong and mighty,"

but I had no wish to repeat the experiment. It had too
medicinal a taste for my palate.

*—Thoreau, in the vicinity of Julian
Allen's lunchground*

In the next few years after Bill and I got settled in at the Cauc
Lake Dam Camp, we explored most of the woods roads in
our area. There were a good many of them—some new,
some not, some being used, some almost completely
reverted to impassable forest. Our idea was to find brooks to
fish and evidence of beaver flowage, but there was always
something to see that took us back into old logging days, and
we kept a game count. Then we began to notice neat enameled metal direction signs that said, JULIAN ALLEN & FILS, with
an arrow. Almost every crossroad and corner had one, and
we were told Julian Allen was a contractor who lived in St.-
Zacharie, Quebec, and had a lumber camp not far from our
camp at the dam. We hadn't scouted that way yet, and
besides, M. Allen, his son, his crew, and his equipment came
and went by the Poland Pond Road and we never suspected
he was around. So now, one fine morning, we came to the

Allen camp and decided to get acquainted. Our neighbors!
Only four miles away.

The camp was smaller by far than that at Scott Brook, but
it had the same layout. Housing camps (the old-time bunkhouse was long gone in our time) with wash and shower
camp. Toolsheds, garages, generator shed. A boss's camp
(for M. Allen, of course), and the essential cock shop with
gasoline pumps. And the big storage tanks for gasoline and
diesel fuel. Then, neat and trim on the far end, a snug cookshack newly painted and with another enameled metal sign
that said, CUISINE. Bill said he'd guess that M. Allen has a
brother-in-law who makes signs. There was nobody in sight,
but we could see a light in the Cuisine through the screen
door. When I stepped in, I surprised the cook. She was not
the man I expected. She was at a far table, beautiful as the
Eastern Townships can make 'em, taking her ease after the
breakfast cleanup with a cup of coffee and a thick molasses
cookie. She had been looking out the window and hadn't
seen us approach. The kitchen was shiny clean, and she was
tidy in clean white kitchen uniform. Black hair, black eyes—
what Dr. Drummond immortalized in his habitant verses as
"de nice leetle Canadienne." "Bonjour," she said. I told her
we were neighbors down at Cauc Dam and wanted to see
M. Allen.

She said M. Allen was *au bois* and would be back at *midi*.
Bill and I were on our way to a scholastic confrontation at
Poland Pond with the contents of our picnic chest, so we
didn't wait, and we finally met M. Allen the next day under
which he considered embarrassing circumstances. This time
we were on our way to our annual revisitation to Baker Lake,
and we rounded a bend in the road near Wadleigh Pond to
find a lone man standing beside a pickup truck in a desolate
and despondent posture, as if perhaps he had just discovered
his gasoline tank was empty. This would be something like
forty-five miles from anywhere and in a place where nobody
was likely to pass until some time next week. As I drew to a
stop, the gentleman turned towards us and revealed in doing

so that a door of his pickup had a sign saying JULIAN ALLEN & FILS.

"M. Allen!" I said.

"*Oui*. H'out-a gaz!"

"*Enchanté!*" I said.

M. Allen was not in a comfortable sling of outrageous fortune. Here was the one man in that entire region vast and wide who should not be discovered with a dry gasoline tank. It might, and possibly could, happen to somebody like Bill and me without undue embarrassment, but M. Allen well knew from early boyhood that HIS tank should never cause him laughter amongst the boys up and down the countryside. Ha, ha, and ha, and so Julian Allen ran h'out-a gaz! Consider, please, that M. Allen, the *entrepreneur de bois* who owns ten pickups, seven thirty-two-wheel trailer rigs, loaders, skidders, and an automobile for going to church on Sunday, and has a storage tank just down the road a few miles with ten thousand gallons of gasoline on the other end of a convenient hose—well, mercy sakes alive! M. Allen was in bad shape, and he knew it.

I told him we were on our way to Baker Lake and would pass the word to anybody we happened to run into.

M. Allen shuddered and said, "Non! Non!" and suggested in French that we turn and take him to his camp. I couldn't seem to understand one word he said. It was pathetic. He would shudder again every time he realized people would know he ran out of gasoline. Bill said afterwards that he had all he could do to keep a straight face during all this, because Bill knew that we had a full five-gallon gasoline can in the back of our own pickup, and we never went anywhere up in those woods of Thoreau without it. When I at last pointed it out to Mr. Allen, he hugged Bill and me and indicated he would never forget us in his prayers. We told him to refill the can and leave it by his pumps at camp. We picked it up, full again, on our way back.

The next time we met M. Allen he was again in trouble. We were headed over the bridge at Ciss stream bound, on another of our scientific expeditions, and again he was beside his pickup in the road. He waved us down to tell us we couldn't get through; one of his truckloads of tree-length logs had tipped over, and it would be several hours before the mess could be cleaned up. No, nobody was hurt. He himself was waiting for his derrick loader to come along.

This sounded to Bill and me like something to watch, which it certainly was, and we told M. Allen we'd see him later at the scene of the wreck. The driver of this truck, headed for a mill in St.-Juste, Quebec, had been tooling along without incident when he felt a call of nature. He had accordingly brought his huge rig to a slow stop, had set the brakes, and had stepped down to the ground to relieve himself. Because of the scarcity of traffic in that region, he hadn't even pulled his truck off the road. And as he was engaged in his personal proceeding, he was much agitated to hear the air in his brakes let go with a conspicuous blast of whooooosh! and to his horror he saw the truck roll down the hill, climb about ten feet up an embankment, and then roll over onto the road. I suppose not too many people have seen the result of such a caprice, and we were fascinated. The driver was able to radio about his distress but had to wait until men and machinery could arrive, and now Bill and I were able to hear him tell what happened for the first time. Since his recitation was enthusiastic and in French, we were guided mostly by graphic gestures, particularly that part about taking a leak.

When the derrick arrived, M. Allen with it, the work started, and Bill and I got out our picnic things and set up our table at a safe place with a good view. The tangled logs were picked up a few at a time and laid in a pile to one side. When all the logs were stacked, a consultation was held as to the best way to right the truck and trailer. When that was decided, chains were fitted, and the derrick, which could lift trucks as well as logs, was spotted in place. It was something to watch and appreciate that here was a rescue job New York City probably couldn't bring off, and it was taking place up here in the wild Maine Woods with just two transients to know about it, and a half dozen woodsmen would finish before Bill and I had our dessert. We did pass around our cookie can, but the men thanked us and said, "Bime-bye."

When the truck was righted, the engine started with no hesitation, and the driver had only to take a pail to the brook and get some radiator water. M. Allen looked pleased, possibly as there would be no repair bill. Bill and I were glad to notice that when the load was ready to roll again, M. Allen shook hands with the driver and patted his shoulder. Then M. Allen walked up to our pickup, thanked us several times again, and said, "Au 'voir!"

"Au 'voir," we said, and it happened that we never saw the man again. He's just lucky, that's all.

But the next day Bill and I went to his camp and drove slowly without seeing anybody to wave to. Not even the leetle Canadienne. And we kept on going, because we wanted to see the brow where M. Allen was loading the trucks going to St.-Juste. We found the place and watched while a couple of loads were made ready for the trip. When the trucks were gone, the man who worked the derrick parked his machine, waved at us from yesterday's recollection, and headed his pickup to camp to wait for more trucks to load. Bill and I were smack in the middle of the biggest wasteland you can imagine. M. Allen was clear-cutting and had covered several townships. In spots we could see planted seedlings getting ready to renew the forest, but for miles we could see but stumps, bare forest floor, and piles of stripped-off limbs. Nothing was green—drab, gray and brown. Here would be the place for Henry David Thoreau to stand and deplore the ruthless abuse of the detested lumberer. Blame it on the barbarous ax! But Bill and I, even though this was early in our Retreats, were already informed about the resurgence of harvested forests, and we didn't see just the ruination of God's beauty. Five years, ten years—give or take—green would grow again.

But at the moment Bill and I began looking for a tree big enough to make shade, under which we could set up our

table and kindle the charcoal in our little grill. Shade enough
to sponsor our customary expression of gratitude and permit
the fervent meditation due. We drove maybe fifteen miles
before we found a maple that M. Allen had left in his passage.
It was a decent tree he may well have left on purpose for
seed; perhaps he just left it because it was hardwood. We
were soon busy preparing to begin to get ready to start to
commence lunch. Bill said, "I see they left the light on for
us." He found a snatch of daisies to put in our vawz, and as
he arranged them, I assumed a Thoreau pose and offered,
"Forsooth, Comrade—that is *Chrysanthemum leucanthemum,*
the whiteweed or daisy, naturalized from Europe and now
common here and in Canada. A dainty blossom and fitting
to our banquet of remote serenity."

Bill said, "Just so, and the Vassar girls and boys use them
for their daisy chains."

"Boys?" I said.

"Same thing," said Bill. "Now, shall I open this Riesling
or would you prefer a Zinfandel?"

"The daisy is also the emblem of the Orleanists," I
reminded him. Bill said, "Ah, wilderness!" I was in
agreement. As our feast proceeded, that lone maple was Paradise enough. We placated the immortals, praising whatever
endeavors they contemplated, and in the comfort of the
maple shade we pondered on the miles of desolated wild land
that surrounded us and how a generation would pleasantly
undo everything that M. Allen had so well done. Beauty
would once again prevail to be ravaged another time.
"Would you care for another taste of this substitute for spring
water?" I inquired, offering the bottle, and Bill said, "Yes,"
smilingly.

Then he said, "I think we've got company."

As usual, he was correct. My ears picked up the sound of
a vehicle, and in seconds a pickup truck came around the
bend from the south, and it came right along beside us to
stop so the driver was right at Bill's elbow. Three men.

Nobody said anything.

The men in the truck looked us over carefully, and cautiously, taking in the flowery tablecloth, the vase of daisies, the crystal wineglasses, the silver bowl of olives, celery, carrot sticks, and radishes, the loaf of home-baked bread with the cutting board and bread knife, the dainty arrangement of cream cheese on the slice of pineapple, and the other Waldorf appurtenances of our genteel repast, and then they stared at our tape player, which was offering some selections from *The Red Mill* of Victor Herbert. We could see all this was beyond any possibility of their comprehension. Here, in the devastation of M. Allen, it was as if Hell had erupted all the delights of the Hesperides. Bill and I were not eager to dispel our visitors' doubts.

The driver said, "I guess we're lost."

Bill said, "That is entirely possible."

"We're looking for Telos."

Bill said, "Do you speak French?"

The driver shook his head, and the other men shook theirs.

Bill said, "Neither do we."

It was a magnificent outing.

Bill said, "May we tempt you with some food?"

"No, we've et."

"Too bad," said Bill. "You should have waited."

Then we told them they were going the wrong way to get to Telos and they said that was impossible, because they started from Telos. They drove along but soon came back to say, "Guess you were right!" Bill said, "We're always right." I said, "He's right!" That was it, all in all, with Julian Allen & Fils, the despoilers of our lunch ground. They gave us one of the most delightful encounters in thirty years of Retreats. I fully believe those three men from Telos woke the next morning and never believed any of it happened. Daisies, even?

OUR RASPBERRY PATCH

Mountain cranberries *(Vaccinium vitis-idaea)* stewed and
sweetened were the common dessert.
> —*Thoreau, about his first woodlands meal
> with McCauslin at the Little Schoodic River*

On our first visitation Bill and I inaugurated a gustatory custom
that never palled. The evening we made camp, we manufac-
tured a strawberry shortcake, and as we always brought two
quart baskets of berries just for us, this gave us a happy bowl
of extra berries, which we sugared and used during the rest
of our stay. Our mid-July date caused a squeaker now and
then, as that can be late for native Maine strawberries. Then
came a year Bill had a full docket in the Westchester County
courthouse, and we delayed our annual retreat into August.
Strawberries were out of the question in August. But clean
living and honest dealing yield rewards, and as Bill and I
drove along towards camp, we noticed a raspberry patch
along the logging road which had already taken up fifteen
miles and was about to require twenty more. Thoreau, I
think, did not mention raspberries *(Rubus idaeus)*. Having
regretted at intervals as we drove along that we would feast
without our strawberries, we now brightened up and looked
forward to a raspberry shortcake.

Our first supper has stayed about the same over the years.
It follows "making camp," which calls for arranging our
foods and stowing our clothes and gear, and making up our
beds. These chores finished, we look to see if the gas refriger-

ator has made the ice cubes yet and govern ourselves accordingly. Everything we can think of that requires propitiation for the success of our week is entered on the operations chart and then checked off one by one. Understand that we are not in a Thoreauvian situation where an Indian comes in and chars our food in wood embers. The gas "bottle" (tank) that feeds our Servel refrigerator also fuels our Garland gas range and after dark feeds our lamps. We do not lack, thanks to our generous host, who is otherwise the woodlands manager of the Great Northern Paper Company. So Bill and I take down the dishes and utensils we shall require, and in a relaxed and leisurely manner commence. We unwrap the sirloin steaks, first, and having admired them, we lay them aside in a handy place where we won't readily forget about them. Then I put fat in the French fry pot and prepare the estimated number of potatoes and then one more. (We might have unexpected company.) Bill makes a salad and prepares other vegetables and from time to time reloads the ice trays. He also fixes the olives, celery hearts, pickled onions, cheese nibbles, and other concomitant dainties which may come in handy. Things go along smoothly, and whenever there is the slightest possibility of disagreement, we take a vote and abide by the majority decision. During the same period of early preparation I get down the baker sheet and grease it and mix the buttermilk batter for our shortcake. Seeing me at this, Bill will set the oven on preheat and remove the plastic cap on the spout of the whipped cream squirt can, which is chilling in the Servel. Before it is time to plunge the potatoes into the frypot for their first treatment, Bill will have set the table and arranged his floral piece. It is approaching time to check the propitiation sheet and see if we have missed anything. In this way we have managed pleasantly for three decades, with the one exception of the year of the raspberries *(Rubus idaeus)*.

These are wild raspberries, and they are a consequence of harvesting trees. Harvesting trees is not all bad. I have asked foresters to explain the sudden burst of enthusiasm that brings healthy raspberry bushes into prolific bearing the minute the forest cover is removed but have not really got an answer that pleases me. Some like to say, "The birds bring the seeds." Maybe so, but what birds, how many billions of them, and where do they find all these seeds? For it is perfectly true that Bill and I came along that logging road that beautiful August afternoon, and we passed mile upon endless mile of mature, bearing raspberry plants hanging red with juicy fruit.

We pulled off when we came to a good place and dug two plastic sixteen-quart pails from our camping supplies. Bill took the thirty-five-mile patch to the right, and I went to its mate on our left. Silence prevailed while we picked four to five inches of fragrant raspberries each—more than we ever had of strawberries, And it didn't take long; the berries were hanging dead ripe in clusters. Our hands were stained with bright red juice.

While we were picking, Bill called to me. "What's been rolling around here in the canes to knock so many flat?"

"Bears." Bears like ripe raspberries, and after one has filled his tummy, he just lets go in the exuberance of good feeling and rolls about. I've never seen 'em at it, but folks who have say it's a comical burst of playful joy, and there's a good bit of grunting goes with it. Bill seemed apprehensive and cautious after that, but he didn't happen to meet any bears that afternoon—although otherwise we saw many over the years.

As we continued to camp, after we had enough raspberries, I told Bill the story of E. C. Johnson, who was the only man who ever processed Maine wilderness raspberries commercially. He had a company based in Cambridge, Massachusetts, that was a leader during his lifetime in the production of supplies for bakeries, hotels, and restaurants. If a bakeshop anywhere across the country made apple tarts, the chances were good it got the five-gallon tin of prepared apple tart filling from E. C. Johnson Company. I met Mr. Johnson in quite another context one time, and when he found I knew the Maine Woods, he told me all about his wild raspberry jam venture. At the time his company was making raspberry jam by the tenfolds of tons, and it was its big item. A customer had invited Mr. Johnson to come to his fishing camp at Wadleigh Pond to try for one of the famous blueback trout, native to that pond, and here was Mr. Johnson riding along, as Bill and I had done, through miles of raspberry bushes. We had found them bearing, but when Mr. Johnson came up along, the plants were just in their spring bloom. There was a touch of tediousness to the roadside, and Mr. Johnson inquired what the vegetation might be that persisted mile after mile. He asked when the berries to be formed on these blossoms would be ripe and was told in August. He asked what use was made of the fruit and learned that what the bears didn't eat they rolled on, and what didn't get rolled on dropped to the ground and went to waste. As Henry David Thoreau had observed, this is a workaday world, and Mr. Johnson owned a business. He asked questions, got what answers he needed, and decided to pack some wild Maine raspberries for his bakery customers. He did try for a blueback trout, but his heart was not in it, and all he could think about was wild raspberry jam. (Bill and I never got a blueback at Wadleigh Pond, either, but they're there.)

Before Mr. Johnson went back to Cambridge, he had made all necessary arrangements. He had talked with landowners and was promised access and cooperation. He had his plant manager come to look over some lumber camps, in various conditions, to see if they could be used as factories. He conferred with some Canadians to learn if women could be recruited to come each day by bus to pick berries and to work in the factory. His plant manager decided what would be needed for retorts, conveyors, closing machine. With a thoughtful touch Mr. Johnson bought nonresident fishing licenses for his plant people who would be in Maine in August. Arrangements were made to house his people at Pittston Farm or the Canada Falls boomhouse. By the time the raspberries were turning red, all was ready to go.

And everything went very well. The buses brought the Quebec ladies every morning, the miles of raspberries were picked methodically mile by mile, and a rented storage shed from an abandoned lumber camp began to fill, tier on tier, with cans and drums of delectable Maine wilderness rasp-

berry bakery filling, and every evening, when the Quebec
ladies bussed back to Canada, the supervisors would do some
fishing before supper. Mr. Johnson told me that any way you
looked at the venture, it had been an unqualified success. He
was well pleased, and the quality of these Maine raspberries
was beyond compare. Commercially grown cultivated raspberries couldn't hold a candle. Mr. Johnson took great pride
in being the only man ever to pack wild Maine forest raspberries. But he did it only that one year and never came back
into Thoreau country.

He said there were several reasons, one of which was distance, but he thought that could have been taken care of by
better attention to preparation for the season. More trouble-
some than distance, however, was the frequency of bears. He
said the Quebec ladies had a definite fear of bears, and whenever a bear was actually sighted, or if some picker found a
bear's rolling place, the frantic cry of "Ours! Ours!" would
bring every woman helter-skelter out of the bushes, trotting
like mad for a safe place. Each running woman usually
dropped her pail, berries and all, and the whole crowd would
hightail in fact down the road with their skirts up around
their shoulders. Mr. Johnson said it would take hours to
restore sanity, and after every panic the women would begin
to pick raspberries again but spent so much time looking for
bears they didn't pick many. Meantime the retorts went
empty and the boys working the closing machine would
understandably go fishing.

But while Mr. Johnson didn't exactly say so, I got the feeling he didn't want to tangle again with the United States
Immigration Service. There was too much paper work to
bringing the women over the line for this temporary labor,
and he felt the rules, regulations, and restrictions were
absurd. The bureaucrats in the District of Columbia didn't
understand the nature of the Maine wilderness, the nature of
raspberries, the geography where this was taking place, and,
above all, the complete impossibility that resident help could
be persuaded to ride three hundred miles into the woods to
do a day's work. So the whole thing lasted two or three days

into September, and there has never been a continuing effort
to make raspberry pie filling in Thoreau's Maine Woods.

Bill and I never made another August Retreat and never
had another raspberry shortcake to soothe our wilderness
desires.

Quite some years later, however, when we were back on
our July schedule, we ran into another effort to use this
annual surfeit of raspberries. We had gone to Caucomagomac Landing for our ceremonial picnic, and we stopped to
call on our friend Argie Clark at the Maine North Woods
gatehouse. She greeted us in her usual outgoing manner and
shortly said, "Do you like honey?" Bill said not in particular,
but I said I liked it very much.

"Well," she said, "I'm going to give you some wild raspberry honey!" From her shed she brought in a beekeeper's
twenty-pound frame of honey for extracting, and with a
butcher knife cut away maybe three pounds for us. She said
the honey was made just up the road from her gate. This
astonished me, because that region does not have honeybees,
and whatever propagation is required for vegetation is done
by ants and wasps, or some other natural method I don't
know about. It's the geography and the climate. Efforts in
the past by woodsmen-farmers to establish colonies of honeybees fail, usually in the first winter. Too cold, and then not
enough honey flow to sustain the swarm. So Argie explained
as she fitted our comb honey into a plastic bag.

She had been minding her gate one morning and a flattop
truck of some size pulled up with the setting of brakes, and a
man stepped down to say, "Mrs. Clark?" Argie could see the
flattop was loaded with tier on tier of beehives. The man
introduced himself, and he had all necessary papers to pass
the gate. He was a beekeeper from New Jersey, and he had
just picked up a truckload of his hives down the Washington
County blueberry barrens, where they paid him to come and
encourage blueberries. The blueberry bloom was now over,
but somebody had suggested he might like to try the vast
raspberry patches up in the cutover townships of northwest
Maine. He knew nothing about this opportunity, except that

he would have his healthy bees up there only during the raspberry bloom, and before that climate could kill them off, he'd
have them safely back in New Jersey. He had been back once
to remove honey, and the next time he came he would take
his hives away. It was delicious honey, with a wispy *Him-
beere* flavor suggesting a certain Black Forest schnaps.

The next day Bill and I drove beyond Argie's gate and
shortly came to some of the man's beehives. The area was
very heavily set to raspberry bushes, and they were then in
full bloom. A dozen hives were arranged on a platform, or
pallet, so they were back to back with each hive having access
to its entrance. The air was full of bees. Assuring Bill that
working bees, surfeited with ample honey flow, are not
about to waste valuable time in animosity towards the public, I walked close to the stack of hives, and Bill came along.
Now we saw the fence.

Right around the stack of hives were steel fence posts,
breast high, and two insulated wires were suspended at the
right height. Bears like raspberries, and bears like honey, and
the combination is more than doubly attractive. Behind the
stack of hives was a shelter for a twelve-volt storage battery,
and as I touched my knuckle to the hot wire, I was convinced
it was ample for the purpose intended. Hair insulates some
animals against the electric fence, but this beekeeper had artfully arranged his wires so a marauding bear would make
contact with his nose or a paw, lacking in hair. Wow! There
was no sign that a bear had been closer to honey than that
first jolt.

Bill and I have not been back to that same area to see if the
beeman continues to come. As the forest trees recover after a
cutting, the raspberry plants recede and nectar for honey will
fluctuate according to, but in that country there are always
new cutoffs to encourage new fifty-mile raspberry patches,
and the opportunity goes on and on. At least the raspberries
tell us the despoiling ax isn't all bad. Don't think ax! Think
raspberry shortcake.

ABOUT THE LADIES

There were also two or three large sail-boats in port.
These beginnings of commerce on a lake in the wilderness are very interesting. There were but few passengers, and not one female among them.
                    —*Thoreau, about to embark at green-*
                    ville on Moosehead Lake, bound for his
                    "Maine Woods"

Even into the mid-1900s executives of the Great Northern Paper
Company had male secretaries. The era of equal opportunity
was still up ahead, but the reason for discrimination was not
discourteous to the girls. It was simply that Thoreau's Maine
Woods was not yet geared to distaff attention, and when a
problem arose in a lumber camp, the gentleman sent to solve
it could accordingly take his secretary along without stirring
up unkind gossip. Would you want your daughter to sleep
in a ram pasture with 150 men? Come, come! It was to be
quite a few years yet before it would be normal to find
women in the woods, except perhaps as seasonal bird watchers and the loyal wives of bosses and clerks. It was never a
law, but it was well accepted that women did not belong in
lumber camps. Bill and I were surprised, even at that late
date, to find a lady cook at Julian Allen's lumber camp.

There had been rare and notable exceptions. Back in the
1890s a woman had become famous for Maine outdoor stories in the fish and game magazines. "Flyrod" she signed her-

self. And the long-gone *Bangor Commercial* had a story just before the World War about a woman who successfully concealed her sex and worked all winter with a male crew without being discovered. She was described as "mannish." It seems that after the spring drive one of the crew she worked with was in Bar Harbor, and he recognized her from behind. "Hey, Charlie!" he called, and she turned to reveal herself. She was holding her grandchild by the hand. No reason for this masquerade was offered.

The first woman Bill and I encountered was to be Velma, the wife of Felix Fernald, the telephone operator at Pittston Farm. No doubt the fact that she was his wife as a bride explained why the "No Women" rule was relaxed. Also at Pittston Farm we met Mrs. Long, the wife of the resident cook, Lionel, but it would be a few years yet before we got accustomed to finding the ladies amongst us.

There is a story about a "meatman" who became a game warden and met his first woman in the woods. Every lumber camp had a meatman back in the old days whose job was to keep fresh meat on the camp table. Nobody was thinking much about conservation then, and deer, moose, caribou, and bear were there for the shooting. Refrigeration was a problem, and access from town could get snowed under. When the legislature finally roused and made it illegal to serve game on a camp table, these meatmen were out of work and gladly took the chance to be game wardens. One such, sporting his new badge, stopped a sporty new automobile of about 1900 vintage to inspect two master-big buck deer strapped to the front fenders. (In those days a licensed hunter could take two deer a season, so that was all right.) The warden found the driver, and lone occupant, of the automobile was a woman, and true to the traditions of the woods he made a sarcastic quip about finding somebody to shoot your deer for you. Then he noticed that each deer had been pegged precisely between his eyes, which suggested "jacking." A flashlight, held on a deer at night, will cause him to stare as if mesmerized, and a deer shot under a jacklight is usually drilled between the eyes, at least a circumstantial giveaway. So this meatman warden added, "And jacked, too—eh?"

The lady protested, but got more innuendo, and after keeping her tongue checked for a time, she said, "All right, put your watch in the crotch of that maple tree," and she pointed about two hundred yards down the woods road. And this came to pass. The warden put his pocket watch as she instructed, and when he came back, he turned to look and the Ingersoll dollar watch did look mighty small there at that distance. Now the lady drew a rifle from the automobile, and in an offhand, carefree manner she jacked in a shell, lifted the gun without seeming to take aim, and squeezed the trigger.

That was that. The watch in the crotch of the maple was gone. The meatman warden meekly told the lady to drive on. Two weeks later he got a package marked "Fragile" in the mail, and it brought him a shiny new hundred-dollar Hamilton watch with a gift card. The card said, "Compliments of the Hamilton Watch Company, Remington Repeating Arms Corporation, the Buffalo Bill Wild West Shows, and your friend—Annie Oakley."

Del Bates told us about the first women he had in his lumber camp. (This was even before progress allowed him to bring in his own wife, Cora, whom Bill and I were happy to meet a few years later.) Del said Leo Thibodeau, as employment executive, was much taken with two Irishmen who came in looking for work, and they had good references and good records as teamsters in the woods over in Vermont's Northeast Kingdom. Leo gave them the papers they'd need and sent copies of everything to Del, who would be their clerk at Scott Brook. So Del was expecting them, and they arrived on the very last day of November, with the winter's first big snowstorm settling in, and both men had their wives with them. Shift had to be made, as the men had never heard of Maine's "No Women" rule, and Del fixed them up with two log camps facing each other on the "main street" of Scott Brook Camp. The two porches were maybe twenty feet apart.

Del soon found out that Patrick Muldoon and Terence
Rafferty, the two teamsters concerned, were boyhood
chums, lifelong friends, and adored each other like brothers.
But the two wives couldn't stand each other, didn't speak,
and made a big thing out of being nasty. This developed into
a situation that amused Del a great deal, and lacking other
diversion in the rigors of a Maine winter, he kept an eye on
the two cabins and had many a chuckle from what he saw.

One morning, Del said, there had been a dusting of overnight snow, and the men had already been to the hovel,
hitched up, and gone to the woods. Mrs. Muldoon appeared
on her porch with a broom, and Mrs. Rafferty appeared on
hers with another broom, and they began sweeping off the
touch of snow.

Mrs. Muldoon called, "Aha! Top of a foin mornin' to ye,
Mrs. Rafferty! And how is Mrs. Rafferty this mornin'? Not
that I give a damn, but it's polite manners to ask!"

Which may or may not be a snide answer to the rule about
"No Women"—but I suggest it; I don't insist.

Not long ago, as the female situation matters, a Maine
timberland company agreed to "participate" in some kind of
educational program thought up by the University of Maine.
A dozen students were to come into camp for two weeks,
and company executives would introduce them to forest
affairs. On the appointed day the twelve students arrived,
bag and baggage, and one of them was a girl. Still on the
"No Women" wavelength, the camp was unready. Where to
house the young woman? As a last-chance possibility, the
camp boss was approached with the suggestion that the boys
sleep in the bunkhouse, and the girl might have the vacant
bedroom in the camp of the boss. The boss quietly pointed
out that nobody—nobody—usurped any privileges of the
boss, that the boss is the boss, and his camp—"No, definitely
no, no way!" Who the hell thought up THAT foolishness? The
girl returned alone in the bus to the university campus at
Orono. There is no law that she can't, if otherwise competent, become president of the paper company, but by that
time she will know who is boss in a lumber camp.

The gracious lady of the Maine Woods, in the experience of Bill and me, was Argie Clark, and it will be hard to tell about her and keep focus on our respect and love. In a way Argie broke the fetters for women woodsmen, for when the several landowners decided to heed the clamor for more access to wild country and set up the Maine North Woods Corporation, Argie was chosen as gatekeeper at the principal entrance at Caucomagomac Lake Landing, where Bill and I had an annual academic picnic for the staff and faculty of our Institute of Fine and Coarse Art. We drove up to the gate—a wire stretched across the road. As usual, our coming had been advertised before our arrival, and Argie descended from the porch of her gatehouse to call, "Well, dammit, what kept you?"

Argie was a devoutly profane woman of otherwise high Christian standards. The wife of Jim Clark, a retired Great Northern old-timer, she perhaps got the job of gatekeeper (several men had applied) mostly because she was Jim's wife, and not for her polished perfection with the blue words. The minute you got accustomed to Argie's language, you found her as dear a good lady as you ever met. She already had permanent *(sic)* lifetime passes to the Great Maine North Woods signed for Bill and me, which was as much as a free pass to a couple of million acres of paradise.

Argie was an ostiary who used her authority if need be. Giving her any kind of an argument led to a dressing down long to be recalled with a shudder. She made out the papers, collected your fee, and then lowered her end of the wire so you could drive over it and reach the vacation of your dreams. Each year, for many, she welcomed us, had time to sit and chat, and usually her husband, Jim, who kept a low profile as a mere guest of his wife, the gate boss, would be there hoeing in his little garden, in which he grew many things well, but Argie told us, "He's so goddamn softhearted he won't shoot the bahstidly woodchuck."

Charlie Nelson, who was superintendent of the West Branch Operations for Great Northern, had involved a big acreage of his company's lands in the Maine North Woods project, and he was the one who decided the gatekeeper job should go to Argie Clark. Although Charlie knew husband Jim well enough from long years of service, he had never met Argie, so one day he arrived at Cauc Landing gate to get acquainted. He drove up in an unmarked automobile and approached the suspended wire baffle so the glass of his head-lamps wasn't quite touching. He set his brakes and began to get out. Jim Clark, weeding tomatoes close by, recognized Charlie but said nothing, and Argie, thoroughly incensed at the brazen upstart who dared to become that intimate with her sacred barrier, descended from her porch.

She shouted, "Who the hell do you think you are, and what in God's name are you trying to do to my goddamn chain?" Charlie retreated behind his steering wheel, and Jim, across the road, did some more weeding.

Argie said, "You break my chain, you bahstid, and God have mercy on you!"

Jim weeded, and now Charlie, looking subdued, got out of his automobile. "I'm Charlie Nelson," he said.

Argie said, "It don't make no damn's odds around here who you are: You can't ram in here like a team of runaway moose, and . . . WHO DID YOU SAY?"

Now Jim laid his hoe down and came over. There was unanimous agreement among all concerned that Argie was the ideal person to bring feminism to the Great North Woods.

Argie put in most of one spring in the Bangor hospital but rallied to have one more summer at the Cauc Landing gate. She told Bill and me, "Every damn quack in Bangor has had his hands on me, and I guess they know what they're doing." She said she was feeling well, but she died that September. Jim sent us Christmas cards with the note "Argie can't take care of the cards this year. I miss her."

Bill and I miss her. Everbody misses Argie, dammit to hell.

VENTING THE BREADBOX

> We had been told in Bangor of a man who lived alone,
> a sort of hermit, at that dam, to take care of it, who
> spent his time tossing a bullet from one hand to the
> other, for want of employment. . . .
>
> —*Thoreau, at Heron Lake Dam,*
> *on the Allagash*

The completion of Maine's Golden Road changed our approach
to our paradise in the Maine Woods, and we no longer came
by Rockwood and Twenty Mile, to Pittston Farm and Seboomook Dam and on to Caucomagomac Lake. Which means
that a better and faster route cost us our annual involvement
with Warren Crosby—and others. And Tessier's Store. Now
we went up the east side of Moosehead Lake, past Lily Bay
and Kokadjo and gained the Golden Road by the driki cove
of Caribou Lake.

The west side road, the one by Rockwood and Tessier's
Store, is the more spectacular way to approach Thoreau's
Maine Woods. You see little of the lake either way—
although the roads are never far from it. There's some water
to be seen as you leave Greenville, but no more until you
get to Lily Bay, after which you are at the Roach Ponds and
Kokadjo. So much for the east side. But to the west you get
a look at Greenville Junction and some of Harford's Point,
and then the Squaw Mountain scenery. And the East and
West outlets, where the Kennebec River starts, to be joined
downstream at The Forks by the Dead River shed. But then

you come to Rockwood, where the horizon is dominated by
Mount Kineo, an abrupt piece of rock that first seems dead
ahead but is really on the east side of Moosehead Lake and
you can hardly get there from here. Moose River, which
flows down from Brassua Lake, is a smooth, still bit of water
that lulls Rockwood. There is a state highway from Rockwood, following the Canadian Pacific Railroad tracks to
Jackman, but the important road to Bill and me was the
Great Northern private access to Twenty Mile, Pittston
Farm, Seboomook Lake, and the whole Penobscot River
West Branch wilderness. As we made ready to turn the corner for the one-lane bridge over Moose River, there was Tessier's Store.

Nobody should pass into the big woods without checking
to find if anybody in there needs something. Tessier's was
the place to gas up, get odd things you forgot, and ask if you
can do an errand. There was a telephone line which some
could use to call out their needs, and others could send word
by truck drivers, game wardens, Great Northern people, or
campers and sportsmen. There was usually something "put
up" and ready by Tessier's door to be taken along by the
next one to pass. One year Tessier said, "No, I guess there's
nothing to be taken along, but if you get a chance to speak
privately to Warren Crosby, you might remind him I'd like
a little on account. His bill has run much too long."

Thus we got acquainted with Warren Crosby.

He was the keeper of the Great Northern checkpoint at
Twenty Mile, which is twenty miles from Tessier's Store.
When we drove up to his chain, he came out of his small
camp with a clipboard and welcomed us with enthusiasm.
He asked our names, our residences, where we were going,
how long we'd stay, and gave us the little pamphlets that
urge safety in the woods, tell us to be careful with fire, and
suggest we give logging trucks the right-of-way. (Once
you've seen one, you don't need to be told again!) Then I
discreetly mentioned that Tessier had raised the subject of
money.

Warren paid no attention, but said he was making a private survey, and would we tell him our opinion about the size of a venthole in a breadbox. In this way Warren led us far astray in a nonsensical consideration couched in heavy language, and he pretended to set down our answers in a large black book you might expect to find in a registry of deeds. We found out later (from Del Bates) that this was Warren's topic for the season, and he had caused more amusement and more bewilderment amongst his traffic than he'd get by tossing a bullet back and forth from one hand to the other. In fact, Del himself, hearing about the survey, sent word that if Warren had in mind his own famous sourdough bread, he wanted to make the hole just as big as he could.

We also learned later that when Warren came in every spring to man his checkpoint, he stopped at Tessier's Store to make a cash deposit that would cover his summer's needs. He didn't owe Tessier any money, and each fall Tessier would pay back any unexpended balance. Tessier, by times, tossed a bullet, too.

The woods do this, and two or three folks that Bill and I met in our thirty years of wilderness joy were far softer than Warren ever meant to convey that he was, and so happy we envied them.

One summer Warren announced that Tessier was a swindler: His dry beans baked up chewy. Tessier responded that Warren didn't know you had to soak dry beans overnight. They were the best of friends.

One year the state fish and game people stationed a warden recruit at Twenty Mile, and his small house was just across the road from Warren's check booth. Bill and I stepped across, as we did everywhere, and introduced ourselves. The young warden was indifferent, even belligerent, and we soon excused ourselves and went back to Warren. "Something ails your neighbor," I said. Warren nodded. "I noticed that, first thing," he said. Bill and I were not surprised to find the warden gone the next season, and his place taken by David Priest, the son of an old-time warden everybody respected, and that David and his wife were living in a new house at Seboomook Landing, ten miles farther along. A year or two later we had business with David.

This time we pulled up at Tessier's Store, and the girl on the register greeted us with "You two going to Seboomook?"

"That's us!"

"Good! Lightning knocked out the phone this morning, and we can't raise anybody. Will you get word to Dr. Bahnsteig that he's to call home? A death in the family."

After a chat with Warren at Twenty Mile, during which he volunteered his recipe for sourdough bread, we moved along and came to Seboomook Landing, where we thumped the door on David Priest's home. His wife appeared, and after opening remarks Bill gave her the bottle of wine that is our customary gift to people we like. "Your phone's out," I said.

"Sure is! We got a granddaddy strike this morning, and Dave's been out ever since looking for smoke."

"We've got a message from Tessier's. Dr. Bahnsteig should call home—death in the family."

"Good as done. He's got a camp just below. Lives in New Jersey. He's a dentist."

When you come to think about it, there isn't much more we needed to know about Dr. Bahnsteig. She said, "Dave will be back in maybe an hour. I'll send him right over.

"Oh!" she said. "Thanks for the candy!" Nobody has missed that indifferent warden.

A year later Bill and I pulled up to say hello again, our bottle of wine at the ready, and we caught Warden David Priest at home. He soon said, "I doubt if you heard the outcome of that emergency last year?" David said he'd gone right over to tell Dr. Bahnsteig there was a death and he was to call home, and this shook the doctor up a bit and caused David to offer to drive him to a telephone. He took him the length of Seboomook Lake to Pittston Farm, but the whole switchboard there had been blown out by the strike, so

David drove the doctor right along to Tessier's Store, where he got through to his family in New Jersey. Then the doctor made two or three more calls and told David he had things arranged and he wouldn't go back to Seboomook with him.

"Put it down as a public service trip, and that's all I knew about the matter." David tells a story well and knows when to pause for effect. After a pause he said, "Then, better'n a week later, two floatplanes come in at the landing, and thinking some sports had arrived, I went over to check licenses. It was our friend, Dr. Bahnsteig. Now, that death in his family was his dog; he had a little cocker spaniel, and most of the time he'd bring it up from New Jersey with him, but that time he left the dog home and it tangled with a truck. The dog lost. So here is Dr. Bahnsteig in the first plane with the little dog in a casket, and the second plane is loaded with flowers—funeral pieces that stand up by themselves, baskets and wreaths, ribbons with gold letters, and a tombstone all carved and ready to go.

"Now, I tell you, we gave that dog one rousing sendoff. It was the nicest funeral I ever went to. Everything in the best of good taste. The little mound was completely covered with floral tributes, and after a week or so the doc packed in sod and he's kept the grave mowed and neat. The little tombstone is set in place, and he's put some white quartz rocks at the corners. Would you like me to walk you over to see it?"

Bill and I felt we had only a week, and there were some more pressing things we could do with our time.

David said, "During the war the old buildings here at the landing were used for a POW camp. I don't know how many German prisoners they kept here, but it was more than a few, and now the story has started that this dog's grave is a German soldier's. Fact! I take people over to look at the place. You sure you don't want to see it?"

The road divides just beyond Warren Crosby's checkpoint—right to Seboomook Dam and straight ahead to Pittston Farm and Canada Falls. If Warren found you were

making a first trip towards Seboomook Dam, he would caution you to drive with extra care around the first bend in the
road. His pet moose family, he explained, might be in the
road, and he wouldn't want anything to happen to the little
fellers. Warren had nothing whatever to do with the moose,
but there was a swamp there that could be counted on to send
any number of moose across the road at intervals of maybe
five minutes. Thus speed was kept low, and nobody got
killed picking off "Warren's" moose. But on the way out,
people would ask Warren how he went about taming a
moose, and what did he feed them, and what were their
names. In such ways Warren avoided juggling a bullet.

One July we paid our respects to Warren and the folks at
Seboomook and continued on. A side road invited me, and I
turned to explore, a brook to fish in mind. The road proved
to be a shortcut on our own route, and in a mile or so we
came upon a long-deserted lumber camp. Some of the
smaller buildings had caved in with winter snow, but the
whole camp was otherwise there. It was a lonesome place,
silent. We noticed the "come-and-get-it" was still hanging
by its chain at the dingle, as if the cookee might step out and
tingle it to bring the crew out from the woods. A ghost village. Our eyes on the buildings, they didn't immediately see
the beautiful doe standing to one side, curious as to what this
intrusion might be. Bill saw her before I did. "There's a fawn
close by," I whispered. We sat without a move for some
time, but no fawn appeared. But the doe didn't move, so
there *was* a fawn! It is possible to "talk" a deer, and I tried.

Gently and without a sound, Bill ran down his window; it
had been half open for July riding. There had been no sound.
The doe stood transfixed, never taking her eyes off our vehicle but very plainly leaving her true concern elsewhere. Bill
and I did nothing for over a minute.

When things are right and a deer hasn't been "spooked," a
mother's concern for her fawn prevails. I made something
like a sheep's bleat, throaty and not loud. A muffled sort of
baa. The doe moved her ears, but not her eyes. I waited

nowhere near so long as it seemed to be and repeated. Still the doe held her pose, anxious but curious. Then the fawn came from the bushes, not hesitantly but directly, having full credence that my fake bleat was unquestionably its mother's own assurance that all was well. The doe now turned away and moved maybe eight feet towards the far end of the old lumber camp clearing, looking back over her shoulder to see that her baby was with her. In July a fawn will be, give or take, a month old, so this one was seasonally red with the little spots of a new life. It paid us no heed and without haste followed after its dam. In a twinkling the show was over; the new spruce growth along the edge of the clearing gave no hint of which way the two had gone.

As when a lovely sonata ends and an enraptured audience sits silent before bursting into applause, Bill and I said nothing and knew we had just enjoyed a North Woods symphony not likely to entertain us again soon. After a few minutes we drove along, and it seemed to us the last derelict building in that abandoned lumber camp looked to show signs of life. Sure, indeed, there were drying clothes on a line between the door and a tree. There, too, was a neatly painted sign nailed on a post:

FOR GOVERNOR

LUDGER COMEAU

Reliable Honest

What was that all about? Who was going to see the sign, here on a back wilderness road? Would anybody except us be by all summer? Bill and I waited a few minutes, but nobody appeared, and we drove along to get to Cauc Dam in early afternoon.

The road *was* a shortcut to camp, but we went that way the next few years hoping to see another deer, and then we found Ludger Comeau by his appropriated residence splitting firewood. No question, we decided at once: Ludger was woods queer. The kind to toss a bullet back and forth. He talked all right, but he was lame in English. He was glad to

see us, asked us how we happened to be on that road, and
accepted a can of beer Bill offered. We felt his candidacy for
governor was not altogether a wild idea—as he viewed it.
We were told later that Ludger came down to Maine as a
boy, saved his money, and had a Montreal bank make some
investments. For one thing, he was in an Ontario gold mine.
He had relatives back in Quebec, and they came now and
then. He cut firewood (on land he didn't own), and the company foresters looked the other way. He would pile up wood
and from time to time a truck would come down from Canada to take eight or ten cords back. Ludger was always paid
for this wood but didn't know the money was from his own
account in the bank's trust fund. Ludger would give money
to a place like Tessier's, and his groceries were always paid
for before he got them from a passing forestry ranger.
Ludger had no problems, and all was serene. Some deer antlers nailed to his camp suggested he may have known what
happened to that fawn Bill and I talked to. If a happy state of
mind would make a good governor, Ludger was certainly
your man. Except for one thing: Being a Canadian citizen,
he couldn't serve as governor of Maine if elected. Too bad.

The year before Bill and I began going and coming by Lily
Bay (our last trip past Warren Crosby's Twenty Mile). I
asked Warren if he ever resolved his big question about the
size of a ventilator hole in a breadbox. "Oh, sure," he said.
"Three-quarters of an inch. You can buy the little ventholes,
already fitted with screen wire, at any hardware store. Tessier has 'em."

That was the year Warren had a good one going about
how the Great Northern abuses him. He asked us, "You been
up to the Muddy Brook checkpoint?" We hadn't. "Well, you
should go see how they treat me. They got Arthur Bessey up
there 'tendin' chain, and you should see the layout they give
him! Brand-new camp! And a generator! A new A-C Onan
generator, and he keeps the whole clearing lit up at night like
it was Christmas. Even has an electric popcorn popper! And
here I am and all I get is a gallon can of kerosene oil every

other week and I have to clean my own lamp chimneys. Coupla weeks ago I was down to reading my Bible during my devotions hour with a mason jar full of fireflies! And there's Bessey, who don't own a Bible! I don't know as he can read anyway. It's an open-and-shut case of discrimination and harassment, and I don't know how much longer I can go on under these conditions!"

(Warren was due to retire that fall with rather generous provisions. Bill and I were not to see him again.)

WARREN'S SOURDOUGH

An improbability made Warren Crosby's sourdough bread memorable. As strangers to the Maine Woods experienced the first twenty miles of it, they realized they were advancing into a strange and wonderful region. Suddenly arriving at Warren's checkpoint camp, there wafted to them the cheerful smell of home-baked bread in a rustic context far from home. And to be honest, when Warren stepped out with his clipboard, he never looked much like a baker.

The Starter

In 1½-quart glass or earthenware container, mix 1 envelope of active dry yeast, 2 cups of warm water, and 2 cups of all-purpose flour. Cover with cheesecloth. Let stand 48 hours, stirring two or three times.

To use: Stir and pour off amount needed for recipe.

Then add equal parts of flour and water, stir, and let stand a few hours. Cover and refrigerate. Add nothing but flour and water as used up.

Sourdough Bread

Put 1 cup of starter in a large bowl. Stir in 1 cup of warm water and 2 cups of flour. Mix well. Let stand 14 to 26 hours. Work in 2 tablespoons of sugar, 2 teaspoons of salt, and 2 cups of flour. Turn on board; knead until smooth. Let rest 10 minutes. Shape into one or two loaves. Let rise on cookie sheet 30 minutes. Bake bread 40 to 50 minutes in 375° to 400° oven. Suggest shallow pan of water on floor of oven, and sprinkle cookie sheet with cornmeal. Darker flours may be used; add caraway seed and brown sugar.

"DISHES TO THE SINK!"

Thoreau did not experience a meal in a Maine lumber camp. Herewith a full report on how Professor Dornbusch did, and what happened and how this fortuitous good chance had a most pleasant consequence.

The Great Northern Paper Company was formed at the turn of the century; it was by no means a pioneer in the harvesting of trees in the Maine woods. Once it got established, its commissary immediately became famous, and its lumber camps amounted to the best hotels in the state. But you had to work hard to eat there, unless you were a company big shot on business, or a lucky deadhead like Bill, and like me. I'm pretty sure my first meal in a lumber camp came when I was fourteen, but Bill's had to wait until our "Retreats" into Thoreau country. It would not be his last, but his first was at Scott Brook Lumber Camp, when Del Bates suggested we partake, and we had places of honor with Adelard Gilbert, the boss. Scott Brook then fed about 150 men, but at noon about half of them would eat in the woods or on the road. By that time all lumber camps were fully equipped with modern facilities—gas ranges, refrigeration and freezers, coffee and tea urns, fresh foods delivered by truck, and competent, experienced cooks well trained in dietary matters. The "cookshack" still had the traditional long tables with oilcloth and the long settees that a man had to climb over to get a place at table. A section of the wall was reserved for notices, and some of them were by no means up-to-date. One, dated around 1910, was a notice that teamsters would get fifty cents a day more, starting November 1. There was the same sign found in all camp cookshacks, TAKE ALL YOU WANT—BUT EAT ALL YOU TAKE. Another sign gave the prices for meals to be charged to visitors and transients: They were inexpensive and were to be collected by the camp clerk. Bill and I always offered to pay but had no luck insisting. Del told us he entered our meals in his book but had a bookkeeping symbol that meant "charge to company." We were freeloaders and knew it and were grateful.

The preliminaries to a lumber camp meal are small. Holman Day, a Maine novelist who did a number of logging stories, did one where the "unity of time" was between the cookee's sounding the gong and the seating of the crew. This makes the German word *Augenblick* run over into the next century. When the gong sounded, Del and Adelard got there first, and Bill and I found them already halfway on the cafeteria line.

Now a little background: George Therrien, a lifetime Great Northern man, lived over the line in St. Georges, and he was the company rep at Ste.-Aurélie to handle any problems with customs and immigration, as well as to hire Canadians who applied for work in Maine. His little office was the first building in Maine as you came over the bridge from Ste.-Aurélie—directly across from the United States border bureau. George had some seventeen children, so it is not surprising that when occasion offered, he hired somebody from his own family. Such was the case that summer at Scott Brook, and as Bill and I made the rounds of the kitchen crew on our arrival, the cookee said he lived in St. Georges and his name was Therrien. "We know George Therrien," I said, and the lad said, *"Mon père!"*

So now we had our plates loaded from the serving tables, and we carried them and joined Del and Adelard to eat. If you're not accustomed to doing it, there is a trick to lifting a leg over the bench, coffee cup in one hand and a full meal in the other, and settling down gently alongside somebody already busy. Bill did it with no problems, and as the ancient rule is still in effect—no talking at table—we dined in silence, as did all the others. The Therrien boy had our table, and he kept renewing the biscuit plate as necessary, and because we were at Adelard's table, he brought us our pie, a permitted courtesy for the boss and friends while all others had to climb over the benches and get their own. The meal was soon over, and it came time to rise and depart.

Again, William negotiated the bench with graceful manners, and he was about fifteen feet from the table when young Therrien's boyhood soprano rent the cookshack air. "Dishes to the sink!" he shouted. "Dishes to the sink!" Bill was unadvised that in a lumber camp you gather up your plates and silver and carry them to the sink, where the knives and forks go in this pan, the cups in this, and the paper napkins in a trash can by the door. Young Therrien was the boss dishwasher, and this was his sink. Bill, now enduring the gaze of every man jack in the cookshack, did as advised: came back and took his dishes to the sink. He had become a full-fledged member, with grip and secret word.

In the years to come, Bill and I had many another meal in cookshacks. Scott Brook Camp was phased out, and the buildings moved. Adelard retired; Del Bates retired and died. We drove over from Cauc Dam one July to see where the camp had been, and the new spruce trees were marching in to obliterate the clearing. The Golden Road was completed; lumbering had gone mechanical. Never again would men live and work in the old-time manner. Bill and I suggested to our Great Northern hosts that it would be good to return home after our Retreat by way of the West Branch Logging road, just so we could "inspect" the far end—the western

fifty miles or so. Certainly, and a slip of paper (which I still
have) was provided that would "pass" Bill and me on the
Golden Road. This meant we could come down the Ragmuff
Road through the several gates, turn towards Canada, and
arrive finally at the border at St.-Zacharie. Then we would
be on the direct international road between Maine and Quebec City, and we would reenter Maine at Armstrong and
Jackman. Straight sailing home.

There was a small hitch. The gate at the Canadian line at
St. Zacharie has limited hours, and nobody had told us what
they are. Besides, there is a small formality called a work
permit, a bit of paper that shows you are employed by Great
Northern and have a right to pass. An ordinary passport,
Canadian or Yankee, isn't worth a hoot. Bill and I, you see,
had a pass to use the Golden Road, but we had nothing that
would let us go beyond the end of it. We drove merrily
along, amazed at the highway construction, absorbed with
the beauty of the North Branch of the Penobscot, and
astounded at the extent of the maple syrup groves.

Meantime, somebody back in the chain of command
among our Great Northern friends became aware that Bill
and I, when we got to the boundary, would have to turn
about and return the way we came, which would make us
very late getting home and could be construed as unnecessary
mileage. While Bill and I continued along all innocent of this,
efforts were being made to spare us a problem. By radio,
word was passed along, and finally George Therrien in his
little office at Ste.-Aurélie was able to reach the wife of the
Maine game warden stationed at the St.-Zacharie end of the
Golden Road. George told her that we had no work permit,
and she said she would handle matters.

So Bill and I come along to pull up at the closed, and
locked, international gate. It is off hours, and no Canadian
officer is there. The game warden's wife is waiting for us and
calls us by name. She tells us to pass and opens the gate with
her key. She says, however, that we are "on your own,"

because if Canadian authorities stop us, there will be no proof whatever about how we got there. She said, "I gather you know George Therrien rather well?"

"Oh, yes," Bill said. "He's been a good friend for many years."

"I guessed as much," said the warden's wife. "He gave me a message I was to pass along."

She seemed a mite curious. She said, "He told me to tell Bill to take his dishes to the sink!"

A TOWN IS BORN

> Think how stood the white pine tree on the shore of
> Chesuncook, its branches soughing with the four
> winds, and every individual needle trembling in the
> sunlight,—and think how it stands now,—sold per-
> chance to the New England Friction Match Company!
>
> —*Thoreau, at Old Town on his way to*
> *Millinocket*

There was no town of Millinocket when Thoreau passed that
way. His reference is to the stream and the lake from which
the town to come would take its name. The Great Northern
Paper Company was organized at the turn of the century,
and work started on a paper mill in Township 3 IP, incorporated as Maine's 467th town on March 16, 1901. Thoreau's
route to Ktaadn took him to Shad Pond, which was in Twp.
3 IP, and there he met Thomas Fowler, who had settled in
1830 and was long since the senior citizen of the area. In 1830
Thoreau was thirteen years old. By the time Thoreau found
him, Thomas Fowler had raised eight sons who were all
neighbors around about and in prosperous circumstances.
Thoreau took notice that land was cheap after the timber had
been stripped, and we get the idea that by now Old Tom and
his eight sons were already "land poor," a term more recently
applied to old folks unable to pay their taxes. When Thoreau
did meet Thomas Fowler, the grand old man of Millinocket,
he was by no means established as the philosopher of Walden
Pond. Possibly Thoreau did engage the gentleman with his

mysticism and sapience of transcendentalism, and perhaps he said, "If each man saves himself, then all will be saved." This would certainly appeal to a frontiersman who had made a pioneer home in Twp. 3 IP and had then raised eight sturdy sons among the howling wolves. Let us imagine that Elder Fowler sagaciously replied, "True, Hank—true!" But Shad Pond, although remote, was by no means distant from the world. The Indians had come and gone that way for generations, and since Thomas Fowler had settled, the Fowler clearing had become something of a crossroads for the lumberers. It was a natural traffic center, and when, later, the Bangor & Aroostook Railroad would lay its tracks to Presque Isle, they would be so close to "downtown" Millinocket that a spur track of less than a mile reached the new paper mill. A surveyor who worked on the railroad right-of-way had a dream as he toted his tripod and glass knothole around, and he could see that here, Twp. 3 IP, was a logical place to locate a forest-based mill. Somehow he got the idea to Garret Schenck, who was operating a paper mill at Rumford, in western Maine on the Androscoggin River. The Great Northern Paper Company was incorporated, and a mill came to Millinocket. The Bangor & Aroostook Railroad, alert, soon laid its spur track from the main line and began running excursion trains from Bangor so folks could watch the progress of the mill construction. It wouldn't be too many years until not carloads but trainloads of paper were leaving Millinocket on the prosperous BAR every afternoon bound for Boston and New York and Philadelphia, and wherever else in the country a newspaper needed newsprint. Now would be the time for Thoreau to return and speak his piece again about despoiling the Maine Woods and chopping down the trembling pine on the shore of Chesuncook Lake. He never imagined what Bill and I came to see: the miles of "pile-down" on the mill end of the Golden Road, where pulpwood waits to be taken inside the paper mill. By the way, Thoreau, who bemoaned the fate of good eastern white pine in the insatiable maw of the New England Friction

Match Company, always carried scratch-anywhere matches
on his marches to Maine. Indeed, he bragged about this civilized convenience to his Indian guide and said if the canoe
tipped over in the lake, they could still have a fire to dry out.
The future of Millinocket and the Great Northern was
shortly threatened by prosperity. Down in Boston Town, a
man named Edwin Grozier had lately bought a fumbling
daily newspaper called the *Post*. Mr. Grozier had been associated with Mr. Pulitzer in New York and was starting out on
his own. He was a man of ability, shrewd, and he quickly
put the struggling *Post* in the black and began a systematic
buildup of the circulation. One of his first (and shrewd)
moves was to sign with the new Great Northern Paper Company for his newsprint. He agreed to buy only Great Northern paper, depending on certain considerations in return, one
of which was favorable pricing in a competitive field.

Within a short time the *Post* began to grow. A new delivery system was developed, so almost all of New England
could have the morning *Post* to read at the breakfast table.
Even in far Presque Isle the *Post* arrived before suppertime.
Mr. Grozier began advertising that his *Post* outsold all other
Boston papers combined and then that his *Post* outsold in
Maine the total circulation of all Maine dailies combined. He
bought a new press, the largest newspaper printing press in
the world, and it was used only for the Maine edition. At
somewhere around eight hundred thousand copies a day, the
Post circulation was the largest in the United States! (Mr.
Grozier ignored a New York City tabloid by saying he
meant "standard-size" newspapers.) What was a tremendous
publishing accomplishment in Boston was not, however,
good news up around Shad Pond, back in the woods of 3
IP, at the new mill in Millinocket. Mr. Garret Schenck of
Millinocket now awoke one morning, put an extra shirt in
his valise, and stepped aboard the downstate morning train.
At Northern Maine Junction he changed to the Maine Central, and at Portland he changed to the Boston & Maine.
Being a principal shipper, Mr. Schenck always had courtesy

passes on the "steam-cars," and the conductors all shook his hand and gave him every attention. At Boston, after a night at the Parker House, Mr. Schenck walked from Tremont Street down to Newspaper Row, where all the Boston newspapers had their own Fleet Street, and he went up to Mr. Grozier's office in the *Post* building.

"Why, good morning, Garret!" said Mr. Grozier. "What a fine surprise! Come in, come in!"

Mr. Schenck tossed a key ring and its bunch of keys on Mr. Grozier's desk. "Why, what's this?" asked Mr. Grozier.

"Those are the keys to the properties of the Great Northern Paper Company, including the gates to our timberlands." Mr. Schenck came immediately to the point. "I've had every lawyer in the State of Maine read our contract, and I've got no way out. We can't make paper as fast as you use it, and now you own the Great Northern Paper Company."

"Come, come, Garret!" said Mr. Grozier. "I'm a publisher, not a papermaker. Take your keys and go home and get to work! Expand; get a new machine, or something. We'll work things out. Come downstairs and see my new press. Biggest newspaper press in the world! Prints the paper you read in Millinocket! You do subscribe, don't you?"

So prosperity didn't kill the Great Northern after all. But the *Post* fell on evil days when Mr. Grozier died. It was sold by his estate to a new owner, whose mismanagement caused the *Post* to cease publication in 1954. But the *Post* never used anything but Great Northern paper—except for those few weeks when Mr. Grozier and Mr. Schenck were "working things out."

LANGUAGE PROBLEM

Some years after Henry David Thoreau spotted his trails in the Maine Woods he became an active abolitionist and a lecturing eulogist for John Brown. John Brown practiced what Thoreau preached. Thoreau did not have a long life; he died in 1862 of tuberculosis at the age of forty-five. Accordingly he never knew of the consequences to the nation of the American Civil War. We can perhaps imagine his thoughts about a couple of racial matters that Bill and I ran into as we followed his trails.

The Maine Woods have had few black and white incidents. Maine was a free state and never had Jim Crow thoughts. In sailing days an occasional West Indian might appear in a ship's crew, and even as an officer (Old Cuffee of legend was black), but with steamboating and railroading, blacks appeared as stewards and porters, living in small neighborhoods at the ports and terminals, where they would "lay over" between trips. Blacks were not, seemingly, attracted to lumbering work.

So one July Bill and I arrived as usual to open our camp at Cauc Dam, and on the second or third day we drove ten miles past Loon Lake to have our ceremonial exercises and

picnic at the lunch and camp ground provided by the Maine
North Woods people. Which meant we'd visit with Argie
Clark at the Cauc Landing gate.

Argie was there. She was filling the sugar bottles on her
hummingbird feeders and came down from the stepladder to
offer the customary apostolic greeting. When it was time to
continue from her gate camp down the road to Cauc Landing, Argie said, "You got the place to yourselves this time—
only one RV down there, and it's parked back in the bushes."

Usually Cauc Landing camp and lunch ground is being
well used in July, and some of those enjoying the place had
become familiars. There was one couple from New Hampshire that we'd seen there for years—a couple so taken with
Maine that their New Hampshire registration plates on their
truck were vanities that spelled MAINE. The big RV van, a
Winnebago, that Argie mentioned was indeed well out of the
open area, and as Bill and I unloaded wangan, we saw
nobody about it. It was a huge thing, thirty-eight feet at
least. And that wasn't all. Atop were three bicycles lashed to
a carrier, a small motorscooter, and a sixteen-foot aluminum
canoe—one painted to look like birch bark. The canoe had
an outboard motor bracket on it—something that identifies
the owner as less than woodswise. Disengaged, a boat trailer
stood handy, but the boat was gone—down at the water,
maybe on the lake. Further, a wall tent with the flaps open
was pitched by the Maine North Woods fireplace and trestle
table, and Bill and I could see dishes, some food items, and a
propane gas grill. Bill allowed that our neighbors evidenced
affluence, and by that time we were waiting for our briquettes to show gray and we had the essentials of our
impending nourishment laid out and poured. "Give you
thirty minutes to the first invocation," I said, and Bill looked
at his watch and said, "I'll hold you to that!" So it was more
or less eleven thirty, and we were back at Cauc Landing once
again and joyful. The day was superb. A high sun, but not
too warm for July; a westerly breeze from the Canadian side
had the trees to negotiate, and by the time it got to us it was

just enough to keep the smoke from our grill on the move and discourage stray blackflies, if any. William was slicing more snack cheese and remarking that this was a very good blue when the door of the adjacent Winnebago opened and a lady stepped out to stand amongst her kitchen-tent items and look down the lake. She made no effort to notice us; she did not speak. Awhile she stood, as if in thought.

The view down Caucomagomac Lake from Cauc Landing is, Bill and I agree, as lovely as any in our three-million-acre preserve of breathtaking views. There are several small islands, about which a salmon fly can be trolled with more than small hope of success, and then the lake broadens and retains its full charm for ten miles. Our camp at the dam is at the end of those ten miles, but the lake curves by the outlet so we can't see the camp. Bill and I followed the gaze of the Winnebago woman and once again again approved and enjoyed. It is a favorite place.

The woman was black.

When Bill and I compared notes later, we agreed this did not surprise us so much as it pleased us. She was, we agreed, an attractive person, slim and well shaped (she was wearing a print cotton playsuit and had a pro-style chef's apron, and she was certainly no more than thirty-five, if that. She continued to gaze down the lake, continued to ignore us, so nearby, and then turned to her table. It left Bill and me well outside. Had she nodded, had she smiled, had she said hello, it would have been the right thing to do at Cauc Landing lunch ground. It was not a moment for Bill and me to make the overture. We had things ready and were about to eat when a man and two boys walked up from the beach. Bill and I caught each other, eye to eye. The man was white. The two boys were neutral. The man had the younger boy by one hand. The older boy carried a stick of driki—now driftwood. They made their way past Bill and me without a word—not a nod, not a smile.

The woman greeted them, and they told her where they had walked down the shore and what they had seen. She

showed interest, and soon the four of them sat at the table
and ate a substantial meal. Bill and I heard every word they
said.

While the two boys and the woman picked up after the
meal, the man walked over to join Bill and me as we lingered
with our tea and spicecake. He asked us if we lived here-
abouts, and we told him we were in the dam tender's camp
at the far end of the lake. He said, "Are you alone there?"

Well, yes, you might say it that way. We got some Boy
Scouts some nights, now and then a salmon hunter, and from
time to time truck drivers and game wardens, and maybe a
walking party of grosbeak watchers, but, yes, we were
alone.

"That's great," he said. "We had hoped we could be
alone."

There was a melancholy tone to his voice, a wistfulness of
disappointment. Bill and I realized he wanted to talk.

He had told us he was a career military man. Now he said,
"I promised my wife I'd put in for summer leave and take
her into the Maine Woods. We've been getting ready—house
trailer, boat, everything. Laid out a lot of money. And now
that we're here, we find the place crowded, and there's no
chance to be by ourselves."

You are, indeed, facing a strange conundrum when you
can go into Thoreau's woods and drum up a crowd. Alone?
Here he'd been, the whole far end of Caucomagomac Lake
his and his alone, so very alone that Argie Clark had said,
"You got the place to yourselves."

He said he'd driven to Wadleigh Pond, and then over to
St. Francis Lake and Baker Lake, and then back down to Seboomook, to Canada Falls, and even to Chesuncook Dam.
Just the same, each place: crowded. Here at Cauc Landing,
he said, people were coming and going all the time.

Bill and I offered no comments on his perplexity. We
wondered at the time and discussed it later: Do you suppose
something had happened back along to make this lad more
eager to be "alone" than our Maine tourism experts had

anticipated? The big Winnebago, and all, were still there
when Bill and I packed up and returned to camp. But on the
way out past Argie's gate camp we met four parties going
down to spend a few days and nights in the remote and
lonely beauty of Cauc Lake—to get away from it all and be
alone with the stars and the hootie owls and the wind in the
spruces and, far down the lake, the midnight lament of the
unattended loon.

The other incident does have a smile in it and lacks the
wistful poignancy of the Cauc Landing lament. Leo Thibodeau, the French-speaking employment executive of Great
Northern, told us about it on an afternoon in camp. It was a
pleasure to hear Leo talk. His English was without a fault,
and we presumed his French was the same, but the rolling
St. John Valley inflections betrayed his Acadian background;
unmistakably he was neither Yankee nor Habitant. Leo said
that when "equal opportunity" began to be embraced, somebody in the Great Northern offices (then in Bangor, now in
Millinocket) thought it might be good policy to hire some
black workmen.

About that time another Maine paper company had placed
a double-truck advertisement in major United States magazines, patting itself on the back for preservation awareness.
The advertisement had a picture of a harvested log, straight
across both pages, with a line of people behind it. All these
people played a part in the progress of the log from stump to
consumer, and each was aware of and concerned about the
impact of good forest management all the way. Soon after
the magazines published the advertisement, a letter came
from the National Association for the Advancement of Col-
ored People, asking pointedly why the group did not include
a black. The answer was easy: The way the Maine forest
industry developed, there were no black people to be in the
picture. It was right after that when Leo Thibodeau was
asked in to confer with management about the possibility of
adding a black man here and there, not only as a gesture of

equal opportunity but quite frankly as an answer to a question that hadn't been asked yet. Leo had mixed opinions. First, he wasn't all that keen about the basic truth of equal opportunity. The unions had worked that theme without reference to the color problem, and Leo simply said it was not true that one man is as good as another. At that time Ted Williams had just been taken from the left field at Fenway Park and put in the military lineup, and there was a popularity around New England to justify this by saying, "Why not? Ted Williams is no different from anybody else." Leo told management, "Take Ted or leave Ted—no quarrel from me, but don't insult me by saying he's no different! There's a little number in the book that says four-oh-six; that's one difference!" But Leo said he'd go along with the idea, and they gave him a free hand to see what he could do.

The upshot was a busload of blacks, recruited by a civil rights agency in Birmingham, Alabama, arrived with considerable favorable publicity to Great Northern in Bangor, where Leo and his assistants began the interviews. One by one the boys were asked about the abilities and experiences, and one by one jobs were found for them here and there in the somewhat extensive work force of the papermaking company.

Leo said one of the men took his fancy right away. He said he was a handsome man—"Real Paul Bunyan kind; two good ax handles across the shoulders." He had a happy smile and manner, which would appeal to Acadian Leo. He spoke well and seemed to have a broader general knowledge than the other boys on the bus. Leo said, "We chatted quite a while, and I was all for the fellow. Likable as they come. I wanted to use him right."

Then Leo asked him, "Is there some special talent or ability you should tell me about? Is there some special job you'd like to have?"

"Yes, there is. I've worked with horses, and I can handle a team."

"That's great!" said Leo. "The time is coming when all

forest work will be done by machinery, but it will be a few years, and we still need teamsters. Would you like to go to our Scott Brook Camp and yard pulpwood?"

Leo said the fellow beamed and said he was all for it!

Then Leo asked him, "Do you speak French?"

"No."

Leo said, "Well, that bubble busted! We don't own a horse north of Lily Bay that talks English."

Leo fixed the fellow up with another job, and he stayed to work for Great Northern for several seasons. Made a fine workman, and Leo gave him a good reference letter when he decided to return to Alabama. And Leo told Bill and me, "You see, it's not true about this equal opportunity and equal ability stuff. Go find me another Air Force pilot who can play left field for the Red Sox."

Leo said that he, too, got a letter from the NAACP, accusing him of discrimination about hiring teamsters. "I don't know how they heard about it," Leo said. "In the next couple of weeks I composed in my head at least two dozen answers to that letter, and while each one made sense here in Maine, I figured none of them would mean much in Alabama. I finally wrote a short answer in French: that in future we would be guided by their very helpful suggestions. Within five years we had swapped horses for skidders anyway."

BIRD-WATCHING

Birds and planes are just incompatible.
—*Ed Abrams, chief sea gull shooter at
the John F. Kennedy International
Airport, New York City*

Kennedy Airport, New York's busiest, sprawls on the edge of
Queens, adjacent to the Jamaica Bay Wildlife Refuge, a
marshy area dedicated to life along the Atlantic flyway. Ed
Abrams is employed to shoot birds that rise from the refuge
and venture on the airport's runways. When the airport was
built, it had long been known that a bird could render an
airplane null and void. In this way man relates to his world,
and Hired Gun Abrams says he hates to shoot birds, but there
are planes coming in. If we can't ease the pangs of Mr.
Abrams's disturbed conscience, we Thoreaux can hope that
before long the sea gulls may find a way to shoot airplanes.

Henry David Thoreau, on his visits to the Maine Woods,
asked his Indian guide for the English meanings of Indian
words. *Caucomagomac,* the guide said, meant "place of the
wise old gull." Bill and I found, so many years after Thoreau,
that the wise old gull is still at Caucomagomac—perhaps
because Mr. Abrams is not, which in turn affirms that New
York City doesn't build airports up in the Maine Woods.

There is no statistic showing that a warden pilot or a pond-
hopping taxi floatplane ever tangled with our wise old Cauc
Lake gull. He does have friends, and sometimes as many as
four—no more—sea gulls will roost with him on his private

boom pier off our camp's shore. Mostly he sits there alone in contemplative posture. He doesn't need to fly far to pick up breakfast, as the Ciss is off his port bow and perch prevail there a-plenty. Bill and I step out every morning to check him, and we speak pleasantly and are glad to see him again. Bill and I are indifferent bird watchers and have no idea what kind of scavenging shore bird Ol' Cauc is; we have never taken Audubon along on our visitations, and come to think of it, Thoreau never had much to say about birds—botany, yes, but few birds.

For good reason. The deep woods have little to offer the lovely feathered songsters that abound in open country and even in the suburbs. There are no bird feeders in the North Maine Woods, although an exception would be Argie Clark's hummingbird honey jars up the lake. The same is true for animals, which avoid the dense growth and work the clearings. So we see no robins and orioles, but we do see certain varieties that like the upper townships, and we have our binoculars handy.

One day Bill and I were exploring a chained logging road (the key Great Northern gives us will fit all the locks in its system) and we well-nigh ran over a man and a woman dallying along. They took to the bushes and gave us dirty looks, and we pulled up to apologize. "Didn't expect hikers this far inside the chain!" said Bill.

They were the real McCoy bird watchers. "Good, sensible" walking clothes. She had a floppy gingham bonnet, and he had an Australian outback hat that would hold about a bushel. Each had huge binoculars on neck straps, and each had a handsome blackthorn walking staff. They accepted our regrets for giving them a scairt, and Bill asked, "Have you seen anything?"

This opened their floodgates, and they began a breathless harangue about a red-eyed vireo which had made their day and justified their entire trip from Connecticut. Positive identification—the vireo had remained in clear sight for minutes to spare. Lovely! Lovely! Intensely emotional over

such a momentous experience, the lady imitated the spectacular call of the red-eyed vireo, and the gentleman nodded and
beamed. Bill and I were so happy for them! The red-eyed
vireo happens to be one bird that likes the denser spruce
growth.

Maine has two grouse, both of which are incorrectly called
pa'tridge by Mainers. The ruffed grouse is still a game bird,
but some years back our Fish and Wildlife department put
the spruce grouse on the no-no list, and it is protected year-
round. The ruffed grouse is found over the entire state, but
infrequently in the deeper up-country forests. The spruce
grouse is found only in the more forested townships, and a
lot of people in southern Maine have never seen one.

Of the two grouse, the ruffed takes alarm readily and will
burst into flight with an explosion of wingbeats that often
causes a hunter to freeze in his tracks and forget to shoot.
The bird also flies erratically, and if a hunter does connect,
he can give some credit to pure luck. The other grouse, the
spruce grouse, has little fear of man and behaves so stupidly
he has the spare name of "fool hen." Instead of exploding in
flight, the spruce grouse will sit attentively and look at you.
When they were still classed as game birds, hunters could
take time to snip their heads off one at a time with deer rifles,
and the foolish things would sit and wait their turn. Boys
have walked up to them and hit them with sticks, even
picked them up and wrung their necks. Luckily for the spe-
cies, the fool hen is not so tasty as the ruffed grouse. They
smack of spruce and fir, on which they feed, and even if par-
boiled all day and floated in onions, they are still sharp on
the tongue.

One July Bill and I were scouting for trout pools, and we
came upon a female fool hen standing by the roadside in
something of a penguin posture. Her attention was not on us
or our vehicle; she was looking into the tall grass by the roadside. We stopped within five feet of her and shut off the ignition. She stood motionless for a good five muntes and
clucked. At this a chick appeared from the grass, and the old

lady clucked it across the road to the tall grass on the other side. In July the babies are fully fledged and able to fly, so it was comical to watch the intense drama of walking the baby over the way.

Now the mother turned back and stood again as before, waiting for a second chick to appear, as it did in another five minutes or so. Bill and I had no thoughts of missing any of the show. We sat there while Mother chaperoned her family of eight little ones from tall grass to tall grass, making sure each in turn wasn't about to be waylaid by a fox or worse. Bill and I realized that number eight would be the last because when it was safely on the other side, Mother showed relief and relaxed her close attention. She had at least kept count. Then she came down from her penguin stance, looking again like a grouse, and she stepped to the center of the road, happy in the accomplishment. Then she took off and flew into the woods, and all eight little ones rose from the grass and flew after her. On other July occasions Bill and I saw this same crossing exercise repeated, but eight chicks were the most at one time. The bird book says the spruce grouse can have as many as fourteen wee ones in a clutch, which would mean about two hours to cross a road the whole family could fly over in three seconds.

Another bird never seen in civilization is the gorby, which the Iroquois Indians named the whisky jack, but not after Jack Daniel's. It is the Canada jay, cousin of the blue and about the same size and shape. Gorbies are "lucky" and supposed to be the residual spirits of departed warriors. It is inviting disaster to harm one, in a highland version of the albatross myth. Stories are told of how gorbies led lost hunters to safety, even in blinding snowstorms. Not necessarily preposterous, since gorbies are also known as camp robbers and scavenge at lumber camp dingles; a lost hunter could follow a gorby in a snowstorm without realizing the gorby was going in that direction anyway.

One July Bill said, "Odd we haven't seen a gorby already."

I suggested he should step out on the camp porch with a saltine in his hand, and a gorby was waiting for him. A saltine will have a gorby on your shoulder, or even on your hand, in seconds. You have to go into the sprucewood forests to see a whisky jack.

For many summers Bill and I had two pairs of bald eagles to entertain us, sweeping in circles high in the sky over Cauc Lake. One year we had three pairs. A game warden assured us the Audubon Society hadn't counted the Cauc Lake eagles. Fish hawks and eagles don't get along, but we did have ospreys, too, and they kept their distance from the eagle "turf." One July Bill and I lunched on the sandy beach at Black Point, west side of Cauc Lake, and it was monotonous to watch a pair of fish hawks splash for some kind of sunfish schooling offshore. Coming straight down from a good height, they'd hit the water with a thwock we could hear ashore, and after each thwock there would be a flight off over the woods—no doubt to feed the young. When we got home, we were going to look in the book to see if fish hawks nest in January, like owls, but we forgot to look.

As with the bald eagle, the Audubons urge care for the common loon, but Bill and I offer an opinion that the loon is doing better than the Audubons suppose. We think the loon has adapted and is on the increase; we've had game wardens agree with us. A generation ago loons lived rather much a pair to a lake. Bigger lakes might support two pairs, but each pair would keep its distance. Then some idiot thought up the 50 hp outboard motor, and conditions changed. The loon is a fish-eating bird, taking its food by diving in pursuit. It swims with both webbed feet and wings. The loon is a large bird, goose size, and its great skill in the water is lost when on land. It is said to have "weak" feet. So when Momma Loon goes ashore at the right season to nest, she doesn't walk around much but lays her eggs right close to the water. So near the water's edge that she just h'ists her wet tail and settles over her clutch, a loon's clutch being one or two eggs a year—never more.

So now comes the sporty nincompoop who believes religiously in the environment and recycles all his funny books, and he tools a Boston Whaler up the lake with every Shinto horsepower straining at the bit, and there goes a loon's nest! Washed by the wake into the lake and good-bye forever. Our lake, Cauc Lake, hasn't yet been tingled by too much lunacy boating, and the two resident pairs of loons haven't been flooded out—so far! But a couple of summers ago Bill got the binoculars out of the case and confirmed what he thought he saw. Swimming along in a flotilla were eleven loons, in stately progress from right to left, and as Bill passed the glasses to me, he said, "I make it eleven, what's your count?"

"Eleven."

How come Cauc Lake would have eleven loons?"

An hour or so later the flotilla returned, left to right, and we counted again. Eleven.

Our judgment is probably as good as any. We think that loons washed out of one habitat have learned to move to another. Cauc Lake, big enough, for one thing, and lacking speed maniacs, now supports more loons. Loons have learned to live together. If this is true, it pleases us, and impoverished will be the North Woods when the night is not rent with the ha-ha-ha-ha of the jubilant loon speaking to his love in sweet endearment.

Bill and I spot red-tailed hawks frequently and have conjectured that they relate to rabbits and red foxes. The rabbit in this equation is the variable hare or the snowshoe. He changes color with the season and is white on winter snow. In July, when Bill and I see him feeding in numbers on the green grass along the sides of the logging roads, he is brown. In the twilight the hares sometimes kick up their heels in the light from our vehicle but as often will pay no more heed than a glance. As the rabbit population runs in nature's cycle, the fox and hawk sightings go up and down. The red-tailed hawk is a brave spectacle, showing us his red tail as he sails out of a roadside tree at our approach and wings ahead of us and out of sight. At twilight, when he is selecting a bunny below his perch and is startled by our approach, we think he makes some cry as he flies down the road. Well, we've been watching the hares graze all along the road a rod or so apart, and then we see a red-tailed hawk and for the next mile there are no rabbits. Elementary, dear Watson! Then we begin to see rabbits again, eating grass. The sighting of red foxes is always more frequent in areas with high bunny counts.

So if we lack certain friendly feathered birds in the deeper woods, we do have others to watch that won't appear at the bird feeders yonder. The greatest show Bill and I ever attended was put on by a cock o' the woods. We had a couple of sandwiches apiece in our pockets and had tried once again to snag a trout from the Scott Brook pool nearest the road. It is a handsome pool, inviting the angler to rest, and it looks as if it will respond lavishly. It never had. Upstream and downstream the little riffles will sometimes offer a panfish, but we never got any welcome at the beautiful pool. Bill and I agreed: Some July conditions would be right; we had only to keep trying until we connected.

This was the year and this the happy morn. Bill scrambled down from the roadway on one side, I on the other, and at first casts we knew that clean living and upright conduct draw their just rewards. We took enough for breakfast and then lolled on a grassy bank for our sandwiches. To one side of us we shortly noticed a considerable pile of chips, as if somebody had taken down a good-sized tree with a chain saw. But there was no stump. Looking up, I saw the answer. "Pileated woodpecker," I told Bill. *(Ceophbeus pileatus abieticola.)*

Bill said, "I always wondered how that was pronounced." The big redhead is the size of a crow, and the largest of the woodpeckers we see in Maine. He's a handsome beast, but another of the deep woods set. He pays little attention to man, and to prove this, the rascal arrived as we looked up at the dead limb of a maple almost over our heads. He had been working this dead limb earlier; this accounted for the pile of chips on the ground. Thoreau never saw a chain saw, but a pileated woodpecker could have shown him how one would work when it was invented. Without any preliminaries, Buster Butthead went right to work where he had left off, and the air was full of new chips that fell to enlarge the pile on the ground. The dead maple limb had turned punky with the weather and came apart easily as the bird's long and sharp beak worked at it with trip-hammer speed and effect. July would be late for a nesting hole, so Bill and I improvised that this cock o' the woods was after bugs—digging out his dinner. After perhaps a half hour the bird flew away, and Bill and I agreed there could be no finer bird-watching spectacle than the one we had just enjoyed.

THE MAINE MOOSE

I trust that I may have a better excuse for killing a moose
than that I may hang my hat on his horns.
                                        —*Thoreau, approaching Chesuncook
                                        Lake*

The visitor to Maine goes home feeling cheated if he hasn't
sighted the lordly moose. I was interested while reading
Thoreau years ago that he didn't sight one immediately; it
was on his second visit and he saw a cow and calf. It's pretty
hard nowadays to go into the wilderness part of Maine and
not see one. In places the moose is a highway hazard, and
prudence suggests it is well not to run your vehicle into a
hunk of meat that may weigh half a ton. Not only do moose
crumple an automobile on impact, but they have a way of
setting up booby traps. Well, homeward bound from one of
our annual Retreats, Bill and I came down past Lily Bay with
our usual regrets for the end of a stimulating academic experience, and rounding a bend in the state highway, we came
upon a wild scene of hectic disorder, and except for my alert
response to an emergency we might have died in a bloody
splash with some three hundred witnesses. In a boggy pool
just off the pavement a hefty bull moose (this one would
dress out about twelve hundred pounds) was standing with-
ers deep in the water, dredging pond lilies attentively, and
completely unaware that the three hundred-odd witnesses
were present. Some passer had spotted him through the small

growth, and then the crowd collected. At a moose sighting like this highway safety is completely abandoned. The first vehicle did not pull off the road but simply stopped right where it was. Then the occupants got out with cameras and video machines, and the next two automobiles, one coming from Lily Bay and the other going, stopped so all hands could get out and look. And so on. Bill and I would maybe be in the twentieth vehicle, and we found nineteen cars all over the road on a bad curve, with all the passengers with cameras and recorders milling around, and an indifferent moose posing his head off in all directions. Bill and I carefully braked down and worked our way through the crowd and the abandoned automobiles and drove on wondering about the guardian angel and why we hadn't been killed.

The great seal of the State of Maine shows a bull moose recumbent under a pine tree, flanked by a fisherman and a farmer. But in truth, the Maine moose has been treated shabbily by the people of Maine, who should be ashamed of themselves many times over. It's not really a pretty story.

Thoreau in his time conjectured that one day the Maine moose might become extinct. It is an animal left over from a previous age, and as everthing has its time and its season, the moose may be farther along in his book than some other varieties of humor. Assuming Thoreau was right, I hope that when mankind also reaches the brink of forever, at least one still-sentient moose is able to rouse and watch man depart with whatever is moose talk for ha-ha-ha-ha. It was in the 1920s that man, by his mismanagement of his wilderness assets, allowed an overkill to bring the Maine moose within a handbreadth of Thoreau's predicted extinction.

A game count is no more than an educated guess. Did we see seventeen moose this forenoon, or did we see one moose seventeen times? We didn't have, at that time, any wildlife biologists who could count over ten without removing a shoe, but the word suddenly went about that the total moose herd in Maine was about seventy pairs. Maine runs to about thirty-three thousand square miles, so there was unanimous agreement that if we didn't stop murdering moose, we shortly wouldn't have any.

With the best of honest intentions, the save-the-moose law was enacted. Folks in Maine were delighted to be told that never again would a Maine moose be taken in sport; all moose were protected now and forevermore.

At once that closed-season law was severely tested and found secure. Boston has a fine museum of natural history, and many years ago a set of Maine moose antlers was acquired. There was no moose with them—just the horns, and they were huge. They may well have been the largest moose horns of record. They had been in storage at the museum for years, awaiting a decision as to how they should be prepared for exhibition. It was decided to create a big diorama for the entrance lobby of the museum. Against a background painting of majestic Mount Katahdin, the taxidermist would mount a moose bearing this equally majestic set of antlers. The decisions made, all the museum needed, now, was a Maine moose to be attached to the antlers. Governor John Hathaway Reed of Maine accordingly got a request from the museum director, asking for the donation of a Maine moose suitable for the purpose at hand. Governor Reed felt this was a proper request, and the diorama would call attention in a dignified and cultural context to the wilderness resources of Maine. Accordingly he passed the museum's request on to Ronald Speers, his commissioner of inland fisheries and game at the moment, whereupon Commissioner Speers requested an audience. "Look," he said to Governor Reed, "this is fine, and we should do it, but we've got a watertight moose law that says no-no and means it!"

"Can't we make an exception for the museum?"

"Our moose law wouldn't make an exception for God Almighty!"

The diorama was completed and may be seen today. The huge Maine antlers are the first thing a visitor sees, but the moose wearing them is not a Maine moose. It was supplied by Canada's Province of Ontario, which had not allowed its moose herd to be depleted nigh to extinction and had no stringent moose law.

The Maine law worked. Maine's residual moose went right to work, and in a few years moose sightings picked up. In a few more years moose had become prominent enough so the misnamed "sportsmen" began clamoring for repeal of the ban on moose. We began to get some strange lingo from our wildlife biologists. All at once we heard words like "wildlife harvest," as if the reborn moose were ready to be dug, like a field of turnips. Loaded "studies" ensued, and "statistics" appeared showing Maine would soon be overrun by rampaging moose devouring fields of corn. Children wouldn't be safe in their backyards. The Maine Sportsman's Alliance, taking due credit for "saving" the moose, now circulated petitions to have him returned into his decline. Very touching. The illegitimate prevaricators in our legislature, of course, nodded sagaciously, but things got even worse.

When the moose was again made legal prey, he was designated as the prize in a lottery. It's the truth. Special licenses were sold, adding to the hunter's basic fee, and if you bought one of the moose licenses, you could shoot a moose, BUT . . . The "BUT" came on a "drawing," and if your name and number was pulled from the Statehouse Hat, THEN you could shoot a moose. If you weren't lucky, the state didn't give back your money, naturally! So the lordly Maine moose was dramatically saved from extinction so he could be the prize payoff in a money-making racket—all with the sanctified approval of the upright and clean-living citizens of the Pine Tree State, who have a moose on their state seal.

There is nothing whatever about shooting a moose that can be tagged as "sport." In thirty years of regular visits to the Maine Woods, Bill and I could easily have butchered a hundred and more of the myopic beasts. One day we paddled through the Ciss from Cauc Lake to Round Pond, and we passed within fifteen feet of eighteen moose, all of which stood stock-still and gazed at us as we went by. The years of being protected made them unshy, and when you're as big as a moose, you don't need to be shy anyway—unless you're dealing with rascals, and how would a moose know that? Shooting a moose is about as sporting as putting a .30-30 rifle to your own grandmother while she sits knitting in a rocker on the porch, with a pussycat on her knee.

By the way, the caribou had become extinct in Maine well before the near ruin of the moose. That was the perfect example of tampering with the environment. Thoreau, in his time, had been told by his Indian guide that "Caribou afraid of stumps." As the forests were logged off, the particular moss hanging from tree limbs that was the principal food of the caribou disappeared. One day, lacking moss, every caribou in Maine migrated into Canada. That was different. The caribou had the choice of migration and—if there were food—could have returned. The poor moose was being shot to death. This same Commissioner Ronald Speers made an effort to return caribou to Maine, a crowd-pleasing but vain effort. Animals were tranquilized in Labrador and brought to Maine by helicopter in a numb condition to be released on Mount Katahdin. Nothing was done about moss. There are no caribou wild in Maine today. Too bad—they'd raffle some old good.

The accursed thirst for gold prompted our moose officials to include out-of-state money in the lottery. A certain number of innocent moose are offered to hunters "from away," at a small increase to defray expenses, of course. This means that many fewer moose are up for "chances" to Maine residents, as well as further insults to the moose. I suppose we needn't be concerned about insulting a Maine native who blithely lets somebody from Rhode Island come up here to shoot a Maine moose that might be his.

MORE MOOSE

"He said, 'Me sure get some moose.' "
—*Thoreau, quoting Louis Neptune*

In Thoreau's time the native Maine Indian was privileged about
hunting moose. Paleface hunters were partly restricted. Nonresident Indians could not take a Maine moose. Moose hides
made the best moccasins, and to get the leather, Indians left
much good meat to spoil in the woods, although it could be
cured by smoking. A moose is just too big for easy disposal,
however you handle him. Bill and I guess that the moose was
much more leery of man in Thoreau's time than he is now.
Two generations of complete protection certainly didn't
cause a moose to run from a tree squeak. Until the moose
was demoted to a prize bauble in a midway raffle at state fair,
why should he run from anything? Today's moose likely
doesn't hear a gunshot until he hears the one that kills him—
from ten feet away! Let us therefore rejoice that our noble
Maine beast keeps a good sense of humor and now and then
contributes a chuckle to brighten the grim woodlands where
he awaits his gruesome destiny.

The first view of Moosehead Lake is from Indian Hill,
when a rise is topped and the visitor looks down upon the
town of Greenville. With his eyes on the beautiful lake, the
arriving visitor won't notice that he is on a bridge crossing
railroad tracks below. These are the tracks of the Canadian
Pacific Railroad. The eastern terminal is St. John, New

Brunswick, and the line has entered Maine from McAdam Junction, New Brunswick. Then, straight across Maine through Thoreau's wilderness, the "CP" returns to Canada at Lac Mégantic, Quebec, to run three thousand-odd miles to the western end at Vancouver, British Columbia. The CP is considered an important American carrier, and its only accepted function in Maine is to divide the state north and south: North of the CP tracks, if you win a raffle ticket, you may shoot a moose. South of those CP tracks you may, of course, also shoot a moose, but you'll be in trouble if you get caught. Better to shoot a summer resident. Thus, for the one-week moose hunting season each fall, the main street of Greenville is the bloody trail over which successful moose hunters bring their trophies home to brag.

In our thirty years of going beyond Greenville every summer, Bill and I have seen moose we didn't count. I think the first one Bill photographed was at Baker Lake—a magnificent bull that made his daily rounds with the timing of a watchman. He was the one that kept the forest ranger's pet dog in a frenzy. The dog was named Baker, merely because he was the resident canine at Baker Lake, and he had come with his master and lady soon after ice-out that spring to manage all affairs of the Maine State Forestry Service. His responsibilities were enormous, and he went right to work. Shortly, on his daily inspection romp, he noticed a dark and dreadful shape on the beach—between himself and the sunrise—and he knew it was up to him to investigate this intrusion and take all necessary steps. Accordingly he circled prudently, coming out on the beach from a clump of cedar growth *(Thuja occidentalis)* in such stealth that he was directly behind this shape, which he could now see was very like a deformed horse, although a good deal more so. Baker had met his first moose. The moose, feeling with some justification that Baker Lake was as much his as anybody's, continued to dip choice greenery from the lake and chew it while meditating on some abstruse memory gem that had been giving him pause of late. Thus things were when Baker, the pup, woofed.

Immediately Baker realized this had been a mistake. His master and lady, up fifty yards from the shore in the ranger's snug cabin, were having poached eggs and Canadian bacon when Baker, the pup, burst through the screen of the door, taking the door off its hinges, and entered to slide under the cookstove and slam up against the far wall. The moose didn't come in; he just stuck his head in.

When Bill and I arrived in July, this had developed into a daily exercise for Baker and the moose. The moose would start feeding, Baker would sneak up, and the moose would then chase Baker to camp. Every morning Bill and I had to stand to one side while they went by, and then we could see the ranger's wife holding the camp door open for Baker to come in. It was ironic for us to hear, two or three summers later, that Baker, having survived these perilous pursuits as a pup, was done in during the winter by some inconsequential mishap at home in Enfield. A cat scratch became infected.

One year Bill and I had come by Lobster Camp, passed the Ragmuff Gate, and had come to the junction of the old road to Black Pond. Bill said, "Haven't seen a moose yet. We're due to see one along about here."

It wasn't more than a mile that we came upon a cow moose who was standing stern to us about halfway up a rise in the roadway. Bill and I agree that simple courtesy causes all good Maine moose to pause when discovered as this one was and give the tourist time to get his camera from the case, check the film, and make two or three trial exposures. None that we have seen in thirty years has ever hurried along until he or she hears the shutter click three times. And this lady was courteous. She looked in our direction and then turned side on, head easterly. Holding this a moment, she then turned to head westerly. Bill, by now, had his camera poised and had stepped from the vehicle quietly. He held the camera to his eyes. At this the cow moose correctly opined all was in readiness for the moose picture of the year, so she turned again, facing away from us, and then she humped up and made water.

Bill got back into our vehicle and said, "A critic, yet!"

Greenville has been our noontime stop on these Grandfatherly visits, and we've seen several lunchrooms come and go. The first year we looked along the main street and then drove over to Greenville Junction. About halfway to the junction we thus found our favorite eating place of all time—not too imposing in appearance, certainly not overwhelmingly inviting, but the sign across the front was irresistible. It said, SOME OTHER PLACE. How many times have you heard, "This time let's try some other place!" Bill and I stepped in to find a prominent sign on the counter, BEER ON DRAFT, and across the counter was a smiling young lady paring potatoes, as in French fries. Bill said, "Only some other place would fry its own!"

The young lady laid down her paring knife, wiped her hands on her apron, and asked, "How d'ya want y'r hamburgers?"

Bill said, "With a schooner of suds and home-fried Eff-Eff-Pots."

Bill and I returned to Some Other Place for a number of years, until the owner and his waiting girls called us by name when we came in and said "See ya next time!" when we left. The French fries were always from scratch, and we had no reason to look about Greenville for—well, I was about to say some other place. Then one July we approached, and there was a new sign on the lunchroom. It said, SPORTSMAN'S CAFE. We went in.

The place had "changed hands." We ate, but the potatoes were frozen "tater-state" stuff, and nobody knew us. Why would a restaurateur, buying a top-notch restaurant named Some Other Place cut his own throat by changing the name to Sportsman's Cafe? Bill and I checked a year later: The Sportsman's Cafe was closed and boarded up.

We had, meantime, found the Boom Chain Restaurant on

the main street and had told the Hollander girl who took our orders that she could call us Bill and John. She said nobody at the Boom Chain Restaurant liked to peel potatoes, and Bill said, "Maybe you should step up the road and see what happened to Some Other Place." Then he said, "I don't see any boom chain."

The Boom Chain Restaurant did not have a boom chain.

A year later Bill and I carried in, dead weight, about eighty pounds of authentic Caucomagomac Lake boom chain, as abandoned when river driving ceased, and in a fitting small ceremony we suspended the anachronism from an eye screw we twisted into the ceiling while our Hollander waitress steadied a chair. Bill and I get echoes from that often; somebody will say, "Hey! I ate in the Boom Chain Restaurant last week and your chain is still there!"

On our thirtieth visitation to Thoreau's Maine Woods, last July, we stopped again at the Boom Chain Restaurant, and Bill brought in his camera bag. "I want to get this thing ready," he said as we waited for our sandwiches, and he brought out the various parts, devices, attachments, and laid them in order about the table. "And lookit this!" he said. He had acquired a zoom lens which he said would bring the nostril of a moose up so it would look like the Simplon Tunnel. Bill said, "Well, all the moose pictures I've made show them standing at a distance. I want to get one right up under my chin." The lens looked as if it might do just that. It was about the size of the plate my sandwich was on. Bill checked each piece of equipment, repacked his bag, and we drove along after our sandwiches. Then past Lily Bay and Spencer Bay, Kokadjo and Sias Hill checkpoint, and we were on the Golden Road, just passing the driki cove of old Caribou Lake.

"Oops!" said Bill. "Moose!"

He braked gently and stopped. From my rider's side, I could see past his nose, and up an abandoned roadway a cow moose was standing in philosophical pose, meditating on the finer things, and she seemed not to care for a hoot. She was broadside on, no more than fifteen feet from Bill and accordingly prominent. Bill was running down his window, which is automatic on a button. The action is soundless. With his right hand he was taking his camera from the bag, and with it the new zoom lens. The moose had moved just one thing in this interval; her short tail inadequately switched at blackflies. Now Bill was bringing the camera to his eyes. Now the moose, courteously, turned her head to look at him, and clearly noticing the camera and the zoom lens, she tilted her head and, I swear, moistened her lip.

She was a handsome sight, although a bull moose would undoubtedly point out her attractions better than I. She held her pose while Bill adjusted his desires, and it seemed to me he was taking overlong and was unnecessarily imposing on the lady's patience. Then I heard Bill whisper a profane and horrid word, audible only to me, which I shall not repeat at this time. "Shutter didn't go!" he explained.

The moose, however, assumed all was on schedule, and having allowed time for perhaps two hundred exposures of her starboard side, she kindly turned end for end and exposed to Bill her port. I had never heard Bill use an uncouth word, and the purple profanity now coming from him caused me considerable embarrassment, and I saw that the moose was blushing. Now and then Bill would press the doohickey again, and the shutter would fail to perform again, and Bill would make further editorial comment. The moose kept shifting to new poses and at one moment lifted her right front foot in a ballet gesture, which she held in motionless artistry for perhaps twenty seconds.

That's the story. The girl did everything she could to make Bill happy, and when she walked towards him, he got frightened and ran up the window. She then discovered the headlamps on the vehicle, and thinking they were zoom lenses, she repeated the routine. In the end she sauntered off the Golden Road into the puckerbrush, and Bill sat trembling behind the steering wheel, muttering to himself in a sad, pathetic manner. I didn't say one word all the while.

Bill did examine his equipment later and decided the action of the shutter for the zoom lens required more wallop than he was getting from the camera's batteries. Everything worked well until he shifted to the zoom. Maybe that was it. When we came out of the woods and Bill was home in Vermont, the man in the camera shop said, "I don't see anything wrong—seems to be working fine now!"

Of all our Maine moose in that vast moose country, Charlie was our favorite. He was huge, and Bill and I agreed he was our biggest. First we saw his hoofprint in a damp part of our camp driveway—right in front, maybe ten feet from the doorstep. Then we saw him over in the Ciss, a quarter of a mile from our camp, and he stuck up big and black against the setting sun. He was there when light failed and we went into the camp and lit our gas lamps. Then we heard him trot past the camp in the night—something he did every night. If we didn't hear him, we'd see his hoofprints in the morning.

Bill and I are persnickety about our housekeeping. We never leave dirty dishes in the sink. So one morning Bill was washing and I was wiping, and Bill said, "Well, hello! Here's Charlie come to call." Right by our sink window, his snout less than a yard from our bottle of Joy, this moose stood calmly attentive to see what Bill and I were doing at the sink. It was the first time we called him Charlie. From then on, for at least three summers, Charlie helped us in every way he could. We talked to him through the window screen the way a bird buff chatters with chickadees at the feeder. He'd stand around awhile and then go about his affairs. Charlie, on the hoof, I told Bill, would go right close to three-quarters of a ton. Odd, too, that Bill never took his picture.

But his picture did get taken. This leftover camp that Bill and I have been privileged to use in July has other uses at other times. Anglers, bird hunters, deer hunters, and now moose shooters take turns. One July Bill and I found a clipping from the *Bangor Daily News* tacked to the wall back of the cookstove, and it was about a party of successful moose shooters who were "lucky" at Township 6, Range 14. There they were, the whole crew: the holder of the lucky raffle ticket, his caddy, gunbearer, valet, guide, personal physician, psychiatrist, spiritual adviser, fiduciary secretary, entertainment committee, and the several other escorts and companions allowed by law to attend the lucky holder of a moose ticket. Everybody seemed pleased, and you could tell from the expression on his face that Charlie was delighted to play his small part in such hilarity and joy. It said on the newspaper clipping that this was the largest moose taken last season.

PAT'S BIG CUSK

> My companion trailed for trout as we paddled along,
> but the Indian warning him that a big fish might upset
> us, for there are some very large ones there, he agreed
> to pass the line quickly to him in the stern if he had a
> bite. Beside trout, I heard of cusk, whitefish, etc., as
> found in this [Moosehead] Lake.
>
> —*Thoreau, near Kineo, 1857, headed*
> *for the West Branch*

The Indian was perhaps an early Maine humorist, probably
entertaining about the campfire as to how he pulled in two
feet of the trout before he came to the eyes. Frightened at
that point, he cut the line, etc. By his own words, we can
assume that Thoreau was a better botanist than ichthyologist,
and I'd like to have some Indian put me onto a trout that
will upset a canoe. There are cusk in Moosehead Lake, but
Thoreau didn't have his bird book on fish with him. Several
varieties of fish found in Maine are sea-run. They move from
the salt water of the Atlantic Ocean into the fresh water of
our streams and make their spawning runs at their time and
season. In his authoritative studies on this, Dr. William Con-
verse Kendall puts an asterisk (*) after the smelt, tomcod,
alewife, salmon, trout, and others as required.

But the cusk seems to be two separate fishes that look
alike. We have a saltwater cusk and a freshwater cusk. Dr.
Kendall, a native of Freeport who studied medicine and was
an M.D., never practiced but studied fish and was chief of
the United States Bureau of Fisheries. He tells us the saltwa-

ter cusk is *Brosme brosme*. The cusk found in Moosehead Lake
is *Lota lota*. Somebody told me once the Moosehead cusk is
a burbot, but nobody in Maine ever saw a burbot, and the
matter is moot. The saltwater cusk is a groundfish, taken
commercially along with cod and haddock, and is tasty.
Makes an excellent chowder. He is, in a way, odd in appearance as he has a fin that begins at his eyebrows, runs over the
top of his head, down his back, and comes around as a tail
should and goes right up his belly to his chin. If you've never
seen one, at first sight he doesn't have an attractive appearance. When Bill, having read his Thoreau, asked me about
the cusk found in Moosehead Lake, I told him how Pat Sawyer caught one. Pat and I were angling cronies long before
Bill and I met. It was in 1937 that Pat was invited by a business associate to make use of a camp at Lily Bay on Moosehead Lake, and Pat and his wife went there for a weekend.
They had good weather and the lake was comfortably serene,
and on the second afternoon Pat was trolling while his wife
took a turn at the oars. I notice Thoreau "trailed"; the word
is "troll"—to drag a lure behind a boat. The depth of water
to which the lure is lowered and the speed at which the boat
is moved are two factors of trolling skill, and as the craft idly
moved along, Pat made adjustments and awaited results.

He got some. Nothing to tip over a boat, but enough to
tell him he was on a good fish. He knew he was down deep.
Mrs. Pat, well informed on angling techniques from many
pleasant hours with her husband, shipped the oars and
reached for the pack basket in which she would find goodies
to entertain her while Pat played his fish.

"Going to be awhile," Pat said. "Feels like a good-sized
squaretail." Then he added, "Much as anything. If it ain't a
trout, I don't know what it is." Mrs. Pat looked at her wrist-
watch and said, "Quarter past five."

At a quarter to seven Pat was still playing his fish and
hadn't brought it to breech. Long since he had said, "This is
no trout." When he did get the fish to the surface, his wife
was ready with the net, and as Pat led the fish towards the
opening and she made ready to scoop, Pat saw the thing for

the first time, and he said, "What in hell do I have?" He had never seen a cusk. In the net, tired and quiet, the fish was still, and Mrs. Pat said, "I don't much like the looks of whatever it is!"

In the end Pat gently removed his lure, agreed the fish was nothing he wanted, and his wife tipped the net and the fish was gone. Now you have to know that the big store in Greenville at that time was operated by Harry Sanders, Jr. He had inherited the store from his father, and Harry Sanders III was next in line. At that time Sanders Store sold whatever you needed to live and play in Thoreau's Maine Woods, and you could go in to get a package of pepper, or you could get everything you'd need for a two-week trip down the Allagash River. And Harry Sanders, Jr., had long since accumulated the world's largest collection of stuffed fish. The fish were mounted and hung on the walls over the stock shelves, and many was the customer over the years who came in for a package of pepper and spent hours gazing at the exhibits. That evening, since you asked, Pat Sawyer and his wife, coming in from the lake, decided to go down to Greenville to eat supper at the Greenville House, and they went into Sanders Store to pick up a few groceries.

So Pat's wife called to him, "Hey! Come here! Here's that crazy fish you had on today! Cusk, it says."

So it was. The metal tag gave the date it was caught off Lily Bay, and it said this was the largest cusk ever caught in Moosehead Lake. Pat was never inclined to dwell on his having returned his cusk of that afternoon to the lake. Mrs. Sawyer wasn't so modest. With a sneerlike giggle, such as only a true and loyal angler's loving wife can effect, she'd say the fish Pat threw back was twice the size of the stuffed cusk in Sanders Store.

During the three decades of our annual retreats, Bill and I saw Baker Lake develop into a good muskellunge fishery, and we're told it's the only lake in Maine with these pike. The first year we came to Baker Lake, we were told trout could be taken here and there, but that year we didn't have a boat and we went for brooks and beaver flowages for our panfish. Then folks we met in the area said something had happened to Baker Lake, and it had gone "dead." No trout for some time. Then it was several years before anybody came up with an answer to this. Bill and I never got an explanation from anybody who could be considered adequate authority, but the answer is just that muskellunge got introduced by either accident or design, and they found Baker Lake a good host. These things do happen, and it's often difficult to find a wildlife biologist who wants to talk about it. Some fifty years ago, for an example, anglers at Rangeley Lake began taking an occasional brown trout—a lesser trout of European origin which certainly never found its way to Rangeley by a road map. It's the European brown, what the Scots call the Loch Leven. They grow them for restaurant food in mountain streams and feed them goat meat. George Stobie, our Maine commissioner of inland fisheries and game, had been an early advocate of "put and take" angling. Catch 'em out, and the fish hatcheries will come by every spring. Human error had merely put brown trout fingerlings in the wrong hatchery tank, and old-time Rangeley guides broke down and cried when beautiful Rangeley Lake was forever contaminated.

I have seen muskellunge taken by sportsmen in the Nipigon Lake region of Ontario, and their size is impressive. When I heard Baker Lake already had muskies close to three feet, I wrote a midwinter letter to Bill over in Vermont and suggested prayer. Bill and I have never tried for a Baker Lake muskellunge. They are related to our native Maine pickerel, of the pike family, only more so. They have attracted many anglers to Baker Lake, so that each summer Bill and I find more and more tents and boats and RVs at the campsite at the outlet. The most likely story Bill and I have heard is that Canadian (perhaps provincial) naturalists introduced muskies on purpose into the St. Lawrence River watershed and into ponds whose drainage comes to the St. John. Baker Lake is the source of the St. John River. Too bad, in one way, but the muskie anglers we see at Baker Lake tell us we'll never know what fishing is until a muskellunge favors us.

ABOUT LOUSE ISLAND

I would rather men would ask why my statue is not up,
than to ask why it is.

—*Marcus Porcius Cato, the Elder*

Thoreau missed the trail at Mud Pond and came to Chamberlain
Lake the hard way. "The walking rapidly grew worse," he
wrote, "and the path more indistinct, and at length, after
passing through a patch of *Calla palustris,* still abundantly in
bloom, we found ourselves in a more open and regular
swamp. We sank a foot deep in water and mud at every
step." Bill and I, who lumped all flora under "puckerbrush,"
were delighted to read that Thoreau continued to identify his
botanical friends even when mired in muck and mud. Bill
and I never suffered in the wilderness as he did. Give him
credit. Nothing herewith is meant to discredit or belittle
Henry David Thoreau. That he did miss a trail is fact he
relates himself, and certainly his wilderness was tamed before
Bill and I came to it. Thoreau tells of soaking thunder show-
ers at Chamberlain Lake; Bill and I endured such rippers
from inside a tight wooden camp. Thoreau tells of pausing
on the trail for a taste of dry biscuit and then pressing on. Bill
and I always take time for a leisurely meal that runs to the
sumptuous style, and we linger. Thoreau's arduous hikes
make easier reading than walking; the longest hike Bill and I
tried was the fifty yards from the abandoned horse hovel at
Scott Brook to the beaver dam behind it, and we stopped
twice for rest and refreshment. Probably the heaviest "carry"

we made was to bring out the ten trout we caught.

And it has constantly bothered Bill and me, as little as we've thought about it, that there is nothing up in those wild land townships that relates Henry David Thoreau to the miles he traveled and the scenes he looked at—the Great North Maine Woods that he loved and by his writings made so beloved of so many others. Seek as I have, I've found only this entry in *The Length and Breadth of Maine* by Stanley B. Attwood: "KTD—Thoreau Spring. 3R9 WELS. Mount Katahdin." If you know where it is and go up the mountain, you can refresh yourself at this Pierian source and appropriately think of Henry David Thoreau.

Then again, there is the business about Louse Island.

When Thoreau, guided by Joe Polis, made the canoe trip from Chamberlain Lake down the East Branch of the Penobscot River, Joe took the party ashore on Louse Island on Grand Matagamon Lake, where they lunched. Thoreau did two things that were typical of him: He noticed a pine tree growing close to the lunch spot, *Pinus banksiana,* which was uncommon in Maine. And he asked Joe Polis to explain the reason for the name Louse Island. This time Joe didn't wander off on his usual attempts to make all Indian place-names mean "Place where squaw dipped water" and briefly said the island was so named because river drivers often stopped there on the sun-warmed beach on mild spring days to shake their shirts in a depediculative ceremony. All winter-hardened lumberers were lousy. If, as is more than likely, "louse" really is a good Indian word meaning the place where the squaw dipped water, we can readily assume that Joe Polis didn't know that. Thoreau lunched on Louse Island in 1857.

In 1969 a group of Thoreau folks first raised the thought of memorializing the Walden Philosopher by attaching his name to something appropriate in the Maine Woods. Lore Rogers, the founder of the Lumberman's Museum at Patten, was eager about this, and after much thought the proposal was made to change the name of Louse Island to Thoreau Island. It was a proposal, of course, about which few State-o'-Maine folks had given much thought. We did have, I'm

ABOUT LOUSE ISLAND *135*

happy to report, some solid citizens who felt an island already named Louse Island deserved to remain Louse Island. Let well enough alone. We'd already harkened to the summer folks and changed Dry Pond to Crystal Lake, and there was even talk of finding a good name for No Name Pond. But louse was expendable, some thought.

Mr. Rogers, in pursuit of his desire, went through channels. He approached State Senator Kenneth MacLeod of Brewer, who had just been elected president of the Maine Senate, a position that made him governor should a vacancy occur. Such a vacancy did not occur, however, and Senator MacLeod opted to run for Congress. But he took an interest in the Louse Island suggestion and asked who Thoreau was. Then the Republican State Committee looked into Thoreau, to see if he were a decent sort and kept Christian hours, and in the end it was decided it would be quite all right to lend the position of senate president to the Louse Island proposal. Senator MacLeod prepared an announcement, and a poop sheet was distributed so the *Bangor Daily News* staff would know about Thoreau when the matter came up. Senator MacLeod introduced the bill, and after a committee hearing it was reported "ought to pass." In 1969 that was as good as unanimous passage and gubernatorial signature.

However, there now appeared a gentleman named John Sinclair, who had been silent about Louse Island because he didn't know about the proposed change of name. His explanation of this is plausible. Mr. Sinclair, a native of the St. John River valley town of St. Francis, had been woodswise from boyhood and made a profession of forestry and timberland management, and at the time of the Louse Island proposal he was Maine's most prominent manager and consultant in the woodlands business. You would naturally suppose he would know all about the Louse Island proposal from the very beginning. He did not.

He explains that as a woodland manager he always kept an assistant who handled the "nonsense" matters. Every day somebody writes to ask if the evening grosbeaks can still be seen at Parlin Pond, if it is possible to get to Pokeypowwow

Stream in fiddlehead season, if a road pass can be had for a party of four, with boat and motor, over Hannibal's Crossing, and suchlike bothersome interruptions in the stewardship of a million or so acres. These nonsense details were ably handled by Mr. Sinclair's assistant, who was a man who knew ten thousand ways to say no. When at last Mr. Sinclair learned that Louse Island was about to become Thoreau Island, he went at once to see Senator MacLeod.

"Ken," he said, "it makes no difference to me, and I can't think of a reason to butt in, but has anybody asked the owners of Louse Island if they like the idea? Wouldn't that be a polite thing to do?"

Whereupon the question of just who did own Louse Island perked itself into the story, and the way some of these great tracts of Maine forest have been handled didn't leave the basic ownership all that clear. Several hours in the state land office and the registry of deeds seemed to indicate Louse Island was owned or had been owned by the Pingree heirs. Mr. Wheatland, who would qualify as a Pingree heir as well as anybody, said he had no objections whatever to changing Louse Island to Thoreau Island, but he had some sort of recollection of selling Louse Island quite some years ago. He was vague, and quite possibly it was another island. Mr. Wheatland told Mr. Sinclair to do whatever he thought best.

Mr. Sinclair never made a decision about Louse Island; the bill was withdrawn just before the final reading and was never reintroduced. A few years later in the settlements of the Indian land claims, Louse Island became the property of the Penobscot Nation. It is still Louse Island. In Township 6R8, it is on the lower boundary of Baxter State Park. The end of this effort to memorialize Henry David Thoreau was nicely capsuled by the headline on the Associated Press story the day after Senator MacLeod withdrew his bill:

LOUSE ISLAND

REMAINS AS

LOUSE ISLAND

WHOSE MAINE WOODS?

> The map may inform you that you stand on land
> granted to some academy . . . but you see nothing to
> remind you of the academy.
>
> —*Thoreau, meditating*

Mr. Wheatland's wonderment about the ownership of Louse
Island is entirely compatible with the history of the Maine
Woods. Let me make some remarks about Justice William R.
Pattangall, who would easily have been governor of Maine
except for two things: (1) his wit, and (2) he was a Democrat.
First practicing law in Machias, shire town of far-down
Washington County, he began writing politically slanted
articles in the good Maine tradition of Major Jack Down-
ing—letters home from a traveling plow salesman named
Stephen A. Douglas Smith. Later in his career (meantime
attaining his fame as Maine's top trial lawyer) he wrote comical biographies of leading Maine Republican figures which
were later collected and published as *Maine's Hall of Fame.*
(Somebody asked Mayor Cobb of the city of Rockland if he
planned to run for governor at the next election, and Mayor
Cobb said, "Gracious, no! It's not my turn."

Pattangall did run for governor in 1922 but was clobbered
by the much-admired Percival P. Baxter, who afterwards
bought up the Maine wilderness of Mount Katahdin and
gave Baxter State Park to the state. Pattangall, not as a Democrat but as an esteemed lawyer, was named chief justice of
the Maine Supreme Court in 1932.

Of the numerous Maine public figures that Justice Pattangall treated truthfully in his *Hall of Fame* series, Edwin Chick
Burleigh belongs here. Burleigh was governor of Maine for
two two-year terms, 1888 and 1890, and was typical of career
Republicans of his time. Justice Pattangall wrote:

> Maine once owned large tracts of timberland. Maine
> does not own any timberland now. Mr. Burleigh was
> once without any timberland. He owns considerable
> timberland now. Maine sold its timberland at a low
> price, a very low price indeed. It has since become very
> valuable. The men who bought it have prospered. It
> was sold, in part, through the land agent's office. Mr.
> Burleigh and his father had charge of that office for 11
> years. Some of the land which Maine owned and sold
> so cheap was afterwards owned by Mr. Burleigh.

It has often been said that some of the things Justice Pattangall wrote about Republicans were certainly actionable,
but it was also understood there would be some futility in
taking a chief justice into court. Of all the Pattangall stories
that were once legal tender in Maine, my favorite is about a
small matter in his early career when he was starting practice
in Machias. He had not at that time acquired any statewide
fame but was well enough known in Washington County.

There had been a somewhat fashionable summer hotel
down at Cape Split, owned by a Machias man who didn't
keep it in good repair and who became careless about his
dining room and his guests. It became what the summer season folks called a White Elephant, and the summer came
when advance reservations didn't warrant opening for the
season.

In the middle of April the hotel burned flat—a total loss.

The high sheriff of Washington County inquired for the
owner and was told he had left for a few weeks in Florida
just three days before the fire. The sheriff located the owner
in North Carolina, where he was intercepted by the state

constabulary and told that his hotel had been destroyed. The state policeman who intercepted the owner also had a warrant for his arrest on a charge of arson and papers of extradition. Back in Machias, shortly, the owner of the hotel came into the law office of William R. Pattangall and retained him for his defense.

The state's case was to the point. It held that the owner had placed a cardboard box of dry pine shavings in the basement of the hotel, had set up a candle in the shavings, had lighted the candle, and then had started for Florida.

Lawyer Pattangall had no great difficulty in getting his client acquitted. And the following morning the owner came in again to the Pattangall law office to express his gratitude and to pay the fee. And he said, "I'm forever grateful to you, Patt, for taking my case, and if there's ever anything I can do for you, don't hesitate to call on!"

Patt looked at the check to make sure it was signed, put it in his desk drawer, and said, "Well, Henry, you put it that way, and there *is* something you can do for me, right this minute. Tell me, where in hell did you find a candle long eough to burn for three days?"

That's enough of Chief Justice Pattangall for now, but will suffice to show one way Maine public lands changed hands. In the beginning every township included a thousand acres of "undivided" land which were "reserved." There was a "school lot" to help start public education when the township should become populated. Also the "ministerial lot" to assist with spiritual needs. These lots were to be surveyed and set off when the township became "organized," and one by one they were frittered away—except that they still exist in the wilderness townships. Austin Wilkins, who was Maine's forestry commissioner at one time, used to tell about a "fast one" attempted on him by a pulpwood company. This company owned a certain township in northwestern Maine, and for lack of residents the school lot was still "undivided." It was a thousand acres, but just which thousand acres had never been established. All at once this pulpwood company appeared and asked Commissioner Wilkins to "set off" the thousand acres reserved to the state. An odd request, and while the commissioner had no idea what caused it, he "smelled a rat." His surmise was, and it was a reasonable one, that the company had discovered a vein of asbestos in the township and was making a wild guess that the state wouldn't find it. In short, when the state selected its thousand acres, which thousand acres would it take? The odds were on the side of the company, and if the state didn't pick the asbestos mine, the company had all other rights. Commissioner Wilkins refused to survey, and meantime asbestos has lost its onetime importance. Does Maine or does not Maine own an asbestos mine?

In several places in his *Maine Woods* Thoreau touches on the way Maine timberlands were used to finance education. And not wholly impressed. He wrote that Monson Academy "had erected a sort of gallows for the pupils to practice on. I thought they might as well hang at once all who need to go through such exercises in so new a country, where there is nothing to hinder their living an outdoor life." In another place he wrote, "When the state wishes to endow an academy or university, it grants a tract of forest land; one saw represents an academy, a gang [of saws] a university."

Such grants of land were readily reconveyed to private ownership, and the small revenues quickly frittered away in a manner that hardly applauds the business acumen of professional educators.

Two centuries ago Bowdoin College came into being. Harvard had already become "Old" Harvard, and now the Commonwealth of Massachusetts felt the need of additional educational institutions—one in western Massachusetts and another up in the "District" of Maine. Williams College was founded in 1793, and Bowdoin College was to follow in 1794. To help fund Bowdoin College, some 145,000 acres of prime Maine wilderness were handed over to the president and trustees; the Maine towns of Sebec, Guilford, Abbot, and that part of Dover-Foxcroft that was then Foxcroft are in context. And later, in a separate grant, Bowdoin came to own two full townships, 7R10 and 8R10, which are still on record as the East Bowdoin College Grant and the West Bowdoin College Grant. Gulf Hagas was, and is, located in the East Bowdoin College Grant.

Yes, yes—I know! Who knows anything about Gulf Hagas? East of Greenville, on the West Branch of Pleasant River. Not far from the historically preserved Katahdin Iron Works smelters and the Appalachian Trail. (Kay-Eye, that is, or K-I.) Gulf Hagas is called Maine's best-kept secret, and a mere handful of hikers follow the trail each summer between ice-out and Labor Day to admire the deep gorge that was ground out of the granite by the swirling water of the Ice Age. Thoreau came close to Gulf Hagas on his way to Moosehead Lake, but nobody told him it was there. I walked to it in the 1930s by a handy logging road that has since vanished. The footpath today runs to about ten miles. The Nature Conservancy has managed to pick up a few acres of Gulf Hagas land, and the Federal Park Service has about five hundred more. The original extent of the East Bowdoin College Grant, where you'll find Gulf Hagas, ran to twenty-one thousand acres. Undeveloped, unspoiled, and completely uneducated, the township was recently offered on the real estate market by its present owner, Champion Occidental, for something in the neighborhood of fifteen million dollars. For Township 7, Range 10, that's a nice neighborhood. No doubt deep in the archives of Dear Old Bowdoin the curious could probably find how much Bowdoin College let it go for. Probably Champion would make no secret of what it paid. I do know that after much professional effort at considerable expense, the annual Bowdoin College Alumni Fund appeal brought in a trifle less than three million. Which the college considers excellent.

THE CROOKED KNIFE

> Tahmunt was making a crossbar for his canoe with a
> singularly shaped knife, which I have since seen other
> Indians using. The blade was thin, about three quarters
> of an inch wide and eight or nine inches long, but
> curved out of its plane into a hook, which he said made
> it more convenient to shave with.
> —*Thoreau, watching Tahmunt Swasen,*
> *the St. Francis Indian*

It is curious that Henry David Thoreau had to come to Maine
to see his first crook-id knife. Those knives were common in
the Maine woods, and Thoreau was not unacquainted with
woodworking tools. He had been an odd-jobbing carpenter,
and we hear tell that some of his handiwork is still preserved
in Concord. He did build his own camp by Walden Pond.
During my boyhood every housewright and boatbuilder had
at least one crooked knife in his toolbox and knew that certain work could be done rightly only by his crooked knife.
Thoreau might have explained that by "shaving," Tahmunt
did not mean whiskers. The crooked knife is a sort of one-
handled drawshave, curved on purpose to suit the way it is
used. If kept sharp, the blade will easily handle a beard, but
the peculiar curves of the blade and the handle would prove
awkward to anybody shaving himself.

A crooked knife was often made by the workman planning to use it, and he shaped the blade from a file, retemper-
ing the steel when he got the shape desired. The handle was

likewise shaped to suit his own hand. In use, the knife was gripped in the right hand, sharp side of the blade towards the workman, suggesting that a careless slip might slit the left wrist, or even disembowel the craftsman. In the small kit of tools Bill and I take on each retreat, my crooked knife is Number One. I didn't make my favorite; it was a gift to me years ago from a Maliseet on the reservation near Frederic- ton, New Brunswick. He had used it from his boyhood mak- ing potato-picking baskets. I think in three decades I used it but once—to do about what Tahmunt did. Instead of a brace for a canoe, I made a brace for the camp's screen door, which had been molested by a freak thundershower wind. A camp- ing trip doesn't need too many tools—until you want them. If you have a hatchet, and you should, you don't need a ham- mer. You do need a screwdriver, and since some nut invented the Phillips screw, you need two. Wire-cutting pli- ers should be considered, and if you shouldn't need them for some mechanical chore, they make an ideal lifter for hot pans on a campfire. A small whetstone comes in handy. I always take along a small bottle of assorted nails, with tacks and thumbtacks. What else? A sheath knife for your belt, which almost goes without saying. And some string, just in case. Beyond that, improvise and make do. You can always open a reluctant pickle jar by holding the cover against a rock, pushing with one foot, and twisting. Maybe you'll spill some juice, but you'll have pickles.

When Scott Brook Lumber Camp was phased out, some of the buildings were sold to selected customers for recre- ational camps, and Bob Bartlett got one and moved it to a shore lot on Loon Lake. The next July Bill and I drove over to Loon Lake to see Bob and inspect his camp, and we ran into a comical situation that Thoreau, in his time, could never have imagined. Bob had brought in some friends to help him with repairs and renovations, and they were hard at work. As we drove up, instead of greeting us in joy at this unexpected pleasure, Bob looked up and asked, "Have you got a plane?"

We did not have a plane. But here was this camp, miles from any suggestion of civilization, and on the porch an AC gasoline generator was humming away. A cable ran to a plug-in box nailed to a porch post, and a couple of fellows were running a pine board over a bench saw, making finish for the front door. We saw a number of power tools poised for use, but the rough-sawn edges of the lumber needed a plane, which everybody had forgotten to bring.

"I have my crooked knife," I said.

"That'll do it!" said Bob.

THE SUGAR PIE

We had dinner [at a public house in Mattawamkeag] and
I think I may safely say there was a row of ten or a
dozen plates of "sweet cakes" placed before us two. To
account for which, when the lumberers come out of the
woods they have a craving for cakes and pies.

　　　　　　—Thoreau, upon first encountering a
　　　　　　woodlands sugar pie

Bill and I found that the Great Indian Spirit of Gracious Living
is dependable, and whenever we propitiated him with proper
ceremony, he responded abundantly and at once. Such had
happened that first day that we visited Pittston Farm for a
steak dinner and our introductions to Felix Fernald and Leo
Thibodeau and all their Great Northern friends, including
Lionel Long and his charming wife. At the time Pittston
Farm was a considerable Great Northern depot, ready to
house and feed whatever number of officers and workmen
showed up on company matters. During our thirty visits Bill
and I saw the forestry methods change. We saw the need for
a "farm" that grew hay and summered the horses lapse.
Fewer and fewer hands were needed as machinery came
along. The telephone central office and the miles of landlines
gave way to radio. Then one July we found Pittston Farm
closed.

Bill and I wondered what the place could be used for, if
anything. A lot of buildings, some of them big. The situa-

tion, alone, needed contemplation. The North and South
branches of the upper Penobscot River converged right in
the farm's dooryard, feeding into ten-mile Seboomook Lake.
The South Branch was white water for a couple of miles, and
then came calmer flowage where the Canada Falls boomhouse was located. Canada Falls had long since been remade
into a concrete dam with fishway, and above that stretched
miles of deadwater as far as the Canadian boundary. As river
driving was being phased out, the boomhouse was no longer
important. But just above the boomhouse Great Northern
had made a tenting area open to the public, and in but a few
years it had become a favorite spot until at times it was over-
crowded. The North Branch, leaving Pittston Farm, ran
diagonally northwest, and it, too, headed for the Canadian
line. In years to come the Golden Road would follow the
North Branch right into Quebec Province—a scenic route as
fine as any in Maine, but keep both eyes peeled for pulpwood
trucks. Pittston Farm stood in the heart of Maine's most
desirable wilderness beauty. Cook Lionel Long and his beautiful wife retired when the farm was closed and went back to
their Acadian valley—to live in a comfortable trailer in Clair,
New Brunswick, just across the bridge from Fort Kent,
Maine.

The Great Northern Paper Company shortly made Pittston Farm available to the Boy Scouts of America under a
most generous arrangement, and Bill and I were relieved. It
seemed to us to be a fine way to keep the place from falling
down, and we supposed the fine, upstanding, trustworthy,
loyal, brave, and reverent Boy Scouts would prove sterling
stewards of the extremely valuable property entrusted to
them. Bill and I never heard just what problems arose, but
we saw a lot of Boy Scouts in the woods for a few years,
and they were certainly happy there, and then we heard the
arrangement had been terminated. We did ask a few questions but decided the Boy Scouts are in the *nil nisi bonum*
bracket. Too bad.

Thoreau was right: Woodsmen coming to town like their

sweets. Also, sugar delivers energy, and energy is expended fast under lumbering conditions. Lionel Long, as chef at Pittston Farm, was famous for delicious and delicate cates and dainties to sweeten every meal. "She don' come on no box!" he would say about his butter sponge cake, and there is something precious about finding butter sponge cake on a lumber camp table. Mrs. Long made the sugar pies.

Bill and I decided that while a sugar pie is rightly a Maine Woods delight, it would be proper to consider it French-Canadian. A good many Yankee tongues never learned to like a sugar pie, even after working a bucksaw all morning, but the French-speaking choppers from over the line lapped them up. Throughout all of Thoreau's Maine Woods, Bill and I were assured that the best sugar pies to be had were those of Madame Long. Hers were "open" pies—pastry in the pan, but no upper crust. Like a pumpkin or a custard pie.

Mrs. Long's Sugar Pie

½ teaspoon soda
¼ teaspoon vanilla
½ cup maple syrup
1 cup flour
1 cup dark brown sugar
Pinch nutmeg
⅓ cup butter

Stir soda and vanilla into syrup, and pour into pastry. Blend other ingredients with fingers until crumbly and spread over syrup. Place foil under pan.

Bake at 350° for 30 minutes.

Bill and I never really cared for sugar pies—even those of Mrs. Long. But we always took some of her husband's butter sponge cake. It was fun to eat.

LUMBERING POETRY

> Is it the lumberman, then, who is the friend and lover
> of the pine, stands nearest to it, and understands its
> nature best? No! No! it is the poet; he it is who makes
> the truest use of the pine. . . .
>
> —*Thoreau, meditating curiously on his
> way to Chesuncook*

Thoreau probably had something in mind. Quite sometime ago
now, a poet named Robert Montgomery brought forth a
couplet that went this way:

> The soul, aspiring, pants its source to mount,
> As streams meander level with their fount.

Thomas Babington Macaulay, a gentleman of standing in literary affairs, commented on poet Montgomery's achieve-
ment with the remark "On the whole, the worst similitude
in the world." I beg to differ. With Thoreau's distinction in
mind, and with what Joyce Kilmer actually wrote, I think a
much more worser similitude runs:

> A tree that may in summer wear
> A nest of robins in her hair.

When I was a lad in school, I sat at a desk behind a Miss
Daphne Delue, who had beautiful auburn red hair in long
braids that would dangle astray now and then and sweep

across my plateau of culture. I was fascinated, and distracted, by discovering activity in her magnificent coiffure, and for several bemused days I kept track of various expeditions to and fro until the teacher called me down front and wanted to know why I wasn't paying better attention. Appreciating that the matter was delicate, I communicated cautiously, and that afternoon the teacher asked me to stay to talk. She told me this was something we should prudently keep to ourselves, and that if Daphne should not be in school for a few days, my special knowledge was not something I should make public. When Daphne did return to school, her braids had been bobbed. Since which time the idea of having a nest of robins in your hair amounts to a similitude I consider very poor poetry.

One year Bill and I wended for our cultural pleasures, and arrived at the Scott Brook Lumber Camp to find clerk Del Bates in a sour mood. He came storming out of his cock shop and with no preliminary remarks yelled at us, "F' Gawd's sake, gentlemen, will you take these people over on the Loon Lake road and show them a tree coming down? And don't hurry back." "These people" were a man and his wife. He was a photographer on assignment from some magazine that was fighting to preserve the wilderness at all costs, and he wanted to show how the chain saw was ravaging the eternal beauties that only a poet would appreciate. They had applied at the Great Northern offices in Millinocket, and to get rid of them, somebody there had told them to go to Scott Brook and ask for Del Bates. They arrived on the Thursday, when Del was beset with the weekly payroll, faced with having the pay for 150 men ready before they took off for *le weekend* at home in Canadaw. Not everybody in Millinocket is smart all the time. Del told us where to find a subcontractor who was removing some old-growth pine that had been missed in earlier cuttings—pine that was already four hundred years old when Columbus was a boy and that would shortly be too old to have any commercial value. We learned later many of these trees were already unsound. Seeing us on our way with the photographer and his wife, Del waved a gesture of "What next?" and returned to his desk.

This was not a major cutting, and we had a little trouble finding the place, although Del's directions were good. The area had been harvested of pulpwood some years since, and the pine now being cut was at random spots some distance one from another. We found a parked pickup truck and sur-mised its owner would be a chopper. We listened for a chain saw, but heard none. Then a pint-size short-legged chap came out of the woods, a red crash helmet on his head and a Canadian Partner saw in one hand. He came to the pickup and refueled his saw. We bonjoured, and oui, he was for *couper* the old pine. We introduced the photographer, and shortly the purpose of the visit was understood, and the little Frenchman entered into the project with a will. With gestures rather than words, things took shape.

The photographer was shown the next tree to come down: The stump would be a good four feet across, and the top of the tree went above neighboring spruce and fir. The French-man showed how he had cleared smaller growth that would be in the line of fall and how he had arranged limbs and brush to cushion the shock when the tree came to the ground. A tree of that size, and that age, will crack and splinter itself if allowed a dead drop to the ground. Working alone, the young man had been readying for some time; now the tree would be down in minutes.

There was some "ham" in the Frenchman, but it was to make sure the photographer knew what to look for. He stuck a stick in the forest duff and gestured that this was where the log would be after the tree came down. When the photogra-pher got his camera placed, the Frenchman walked back to check the direction of sight and tried to tell the photographer several things it would be useful to know; the photographer asked Bill and me what he said, and Bill and I assured him we didn't know. I've been told French is useful in ways that other languages are not, and it may be so. All this took a little time, and now we were ready.

"Hokay?" said the chopper.

"All OK!" said the photographer.

We've all seen an artist hold up his hands and fingers to "frame" something he considers painting. So, now, this chain saw artist scanned the job before him. At home, if I decide to use my chain saw, it will take at least six healthy yanks on the struggle string, and then nine times out of ten the saw will cough and subside into silence. But let a Canadian pull idly on his Partner, and the motor will purr like a pussycat and run as sweetly as a sonata until the gasoline tank is dry. Our chopper now idly pulled, and he was ready. He gave a last look up into the branches he was about to bring down, sighted once more at the stick he'd shoved into the ground, and applied his saw to the scarf—the pie-shaped section which he would remove first and which settles the precise direction in which the tree will fall. The scarf popped out, leaving the triangular gash intended. No poet ever metered a line with more fluid nicety! No artist ever drew straighter edges.

Our Frenchman now flipped the on-off toggle on his saw, and the afternoon in the Loon Lake quadrangle fell silent. Once more he looked everything over. The scarf got careful scrutiny, and he was satisfied. The saw spoke again, and he revved the trigger so it snarled and cried, "Ready!" Some say the Canadians can talk with their Partners, as Indians on the trail send smoke signals. The surging teeth of the "shinesaw" bit into the pine bark on the nigh side, and in scarce seconds the sawdust was three inches deep on the ground. The blade was almost through to the scarf. Once more the on-off switch was flipped.

I had seen big trees felled; I had felled them in my own woodlot for firewood and lumber. I appreciated to the full the experienced cunning of this Canadian. Bill and the photographer were about to see this for the first time. (The wife, evidently terrified by the whine of the saw and the deed about to be done, had retreated well out of viewing distance and actually saw little.) So now it came. The Frenchman had so correctly calculated that a simple half inch was enough to bring the saw to the scarf, and he withdrew the saw to step back a good fifteen feet and do the two things woodscraft demands:

1. Shout "TIMBER-R-R-R!" so everybody is alerted—i.e., in French, *tamb-bear!*
2. Look up. Men have been killed by the widow-maker, the stray limb that drops at fearful random.

But the severed tree had not yet left its upright position. Kinetics had not set in. Momentum was not yet in effect. The silence as the chain saw stopped was overpowering. Then came a crack, not too loud, but loud enough to tell us the last splinter between stump and log was severed. Then we could see that the tree was moving. Just barely, and then we could see that it was moving some more. Time has no meaning in those seconds when a pine begins to descend. It can be three seconds or can seem all of a tricky hour before the treetop, beginning to gain motion, makes the eerie sound of pine needles swishing the air. This, in turn, becomes a rushing gale when the tree is only halfway to the ground.

Nothing about all this is like the workaday felling of mere spruce and fir that will be ground into paper pulp. This is like the mighty oak on Mount Ida as in a classical legend. Our Frenchman stood in salute, once again subdued by an epic scene he had witnessed in awe how many thousand times? The falling pine was roaring as, standing, it had never roared in the wind before.

Then it reached the cradle the chopper had artfully arranged to soften the blow. There was some cracking as limbs broke in the collision, but the tree bounced, and bounced again, and then there was silence. It lasted while the four of us (the lady from well back) applauded the Frenchman with full operatic honors, and he had started his saw again to "limb out." He cut the tree-length log to sawmill lengths, and by that time a new sound overplayed his Partner. It was a skidder coming to twitch the pine out to the road. The next sound after that would be the loader and the truck, and the poet would have one less pine tree to inspire his lyre—or his indignation, which makes verses.

The photographer, who had now been rejoined by his wife, told us he was perfectly happy with the exposures he got of the entire spectacle. Bill and I never saw any of his pictures in print. The couple went "out" by the Ragmuff Road, and Bill and I went back to Scott Brook to continue our interrupted visit with Clerk Bates. Del had completed his desk work and was standing on his cock shop porch waiting for us to come around the bend in the road.

"Gentlemen! Gentlemen!" he said. "You tarried o'erlong on a frivolous mission! I'm grateful for your kind cooperation! Which would you rather—wet your whistles?"

That stick the Frenchman had stuck in the forest duff to show where the tree would land had been driven out of sight into the ground by the impact.

NEXT TO GODLINESS

My companion wandered up the bank to look for
moose, while Joe went to sleep on the bank, and I
improved the opportunity to botanize and bathe.
—Thoreau at Lobster Stream

What's a' your jargon o' your Schools,
Your Latin words for horns and stools?
—Robert Burns to an old Scottish bard

By the old road from Scott Brook to Caucomagomac Dam
there's an interesting pine *(Pinus strobus)* that stands tall
amongst the *Picea rubens Sarg.* and the *Abies balsamea (L.)
Miller*—not to mention the *Picea glauca (Moench) Voss*—and
it is impossible to pass without admiring it. It is an anachronism, a true "old-growth" pine that is a remnant of the forests of Maine logged off in the 1800s. With Sappho's red
apple in mind, which the pickers forgot or couldn't reach,
what happened to spare this lonely pine? There are some old-
growth pines still left in our Maine wilderness, but they are
far back in inaccessible places, and none so visible as this
one—close to the road and on a knoll much by itself. This is
what a mast pine was like—marked with the broad arrow of
the king and sacred to his navy. It was the gallows for any
rude Mainer who dared touch the reserved mast pine. Maybe
this one had a defect that saved it. Thoreau did wander that
way and perhaps noticed the very tree. It would already have
size, and even today, if its butt log is shaky, it would scale

out maybe three M board feet. When Bill and I first came into that country, I pointed at that Pine and botanized. "There, Bill," I said, "by some quirk of chance stands a *Pinus strobus l.*, left over from the long log days before pulpwood!" Bill said, "Well, lah-di-dah!"

That, I believe, was the first and last effort of Bill and me at botanizing, and in the next twenty-nine visitations, as we pass the same tree again, Bill says, "Well, lah-di-dah!"

And we speak of daisies and buttercups as such, admiring them just as much as we can.

On the other hand we are authorities on wilderness ablutions. Caucomagomac Lake is ten miles of robust bathtub. Thoreau used it. Thoreau called this the "lake country" of Maine. But the lakes in the lake country of Maine retain a loyal connection to their prime ancestor—the Ice Age. If you wander the shores of these lakes, you will notice here and there little trickles of water that gurgle and bubble and are escaping from underground crevices that are connected on the other end to residual but rectified liquid zero under yonder mountain, where the tail end of a prehistoric glacier mopes in a lingering mood. One of these little springs is dandy if broached on a hot day while a-hike. But in the comfort of a pleasant afternoon, on our folding chairs looking off across the lake, we meditate on the difference between going in and staying out, and ablutions often fail to come to mind. Many's the time we've been enjoying the comfort of the cultural marble patio on our sumptuous museum of the manifold opportunities, and we will see a flotilla of Boy Scout canoes come out of the Ciss and pass before us towards the campsite at the dam. Seven or eight canoes, usually, with a Boy Scout afore and a Boy Scout astern, and a scoutmaster holding down the middle thwart. Bill and I have never seen a scoutmaster with a paddle. The canoes pass in silence, paddles rising and falling in the rhythm most comfortable for the scoutmasters, and soon after the flotilla has reached the campsite, we can hear the Boy Scouts screaming in pain as they take what Boy Scouts call a dip. Bill and I, many times,

have squirmed at the very thought and turn our attention to
the *veritas* that is in *vino* and decide that we can go one more
night without an overall *nettoyage*.

There has been but one summer in thirty that Bill and I
could use Cauc Lake without having our toenails turn blue.
A spell of dry heat came over the land, and it was not
assuaged by the thundershowers common in the woods that
cool down the camp for pleasant sleeping. It just stayed hot.
So hot that one afternoon Del Bates called the crews in from
the cuttings. Del was first-aid man at the camp and was
proud of a long streak of safety days with no lost-time acci-
dents; he didn't want to tangle with an epidemic of heat
stroke. Bill and I woke the next morning to a silent sunrise;
no chain saws could be heard from the Loon Lake operation.
It stayed so hot that the men didn't grumble one bit about
losing the pay. That was one of the years Bill and I brought
a boat and motor, and we spent more time in the lake than
we did on it.

Cauc Lake has "iron" water. Most of the lakes in that area
do have a rusty tinge, indicating a high iron content. Such
water is potable, but Bill and I bring glass jugs and fetch
drinking water from one of the roadside springs along our
way. We do dip "pond water" from the lake for our casual
ablutions and washing dishes. All water in that region is
"hard" and lathers with reluctance. Bill washes the dishes and
I wipe, and he thinks Joy is as good as anything for the dish-
pans. To get trout gurry off our slimy hands, we like Camay.

We plan on bringing enough clean clothes to last, but if
we need to launder a shirt or some pants, there is no problem. We tie a length of fishing twine to the garment, which
we soap well, and attach the other end of the twine to a bush
along the riverbank, allowing the garment to dangle and
swirl in the current all night. A black alder *(Alnus glutinosa
vulgaris)* is as good as a Whirlpool or a Maytag.

Bill, accustomed to more fastidious toilets than I, likes to
shave every morning. He heats some pond water, and with-
draws to the open air with his tools and tonics, and adjusts

the side mirror of our vehicle so the golden beams of the rising sun illuminate his features in splendor. He then entertains the chickadiddles, gorbies, redwings, and other neighbors with mouth awry while humming some catchy tune from Cole Porter or Stephen Foster. I do the same, but usually every third day, and I don't sing, by request.

I believe as fine a wilderness pleasure as a man can have is a gentle shave in the rosy dawn of a Maine wilderness summer day, warm Cauc Lake pond water ready, and birdies a-twitter with paeans to wrench envy from blessed St. Francis himself. All's right with the world.

ABOUT THE WANGAN

> A strip of cotton cloth for a tent, a couple of blankets, which would suffice for the whole party, fifteen pounds of hard bread, ten pounds of "clear" pork, and a little tea, made up "Uncle George's" pack. The last three articles were calculated to be provision enough for six men for a week with what we might pick up.
>
> *—Thoreau describing the wangan as his party set out to climb Mount Katahdin*

Wangan is an Indian word that means the aggregate of food and gear to sustain a brave or party of braves on the trail. There are no mom-and-dad convenience stores in Thoreau's Maine Woods. But today it is not necessary to keep the supplies as austere as Thoreau enumerates. Bill and I had a pickup truck with more than enough room for frivolities as well as necessities, and we stinted not. Our motto was "We shall not want," and we didn't—even to the little jar of maraschino cherries to embellish Bill's evening Manhattans. We engaged in no muscular exercises such as Thoreau's portages with his salt pork, although we had salt pork, too. The difference 'twixt Thoreau and us can be summed up by our traditional first evening in camp, when sirloin steaks and French fried potatoes were foundation for cates and dainties hardly common in roughing it. The strawberry shortcake with whipped cream always seemed a fitting finale, although after a few years Bill allowed the squirt can kind was "about as good" and saved him time on the eggbeater.

To anybody making any kind of holiday visit to Thoreau ground, we suggest the checklist developed over the years by Harry Sanders, who kept the principal store in Greenville. Harry had inherited the store from his father but always retained his "Junior" even after he retired as an old man and left the store to his son. Harry advertised that he sold "experience." And so he did. He was the leading outfitter for folks making the Allagash River canoe trip. Tell him how many people and how many days, and he'd bring down his checklist and start packing—everything including canoes and fly dope. Times had changed since Thoreau was first in Greenville. Thoreau told how the Indians daubed their birch canoes against leaks; Harry Sanders always stuck in a can of shellac and a paintbrush should you have an Allagash rock snap as you went by. I don't recall that Bill and I ever crossed anything off Harry's checklist, but now and then we did add a new item.

Sander's Store   Greenville
North Maine Woods Checklist

tea / coffee	bacon	hot dog rolls
salt / pepper	eggs	hamburg rolls
onions	sausage	cheeses
potatoes	wieners	peanut butter
fresh milk	knackwurst	whipped cream
dry milk	sauerkraut	tinned nuts
tinned milk	cookies	popcorn / popper
mustard	doughnuts	yeast
canned fruit	greens for salad	baking soda
canned juices	mar. cherries	mushrooms
canned veggies	pretzels	plastic glasses

canned soups

baked beans

brown bread

beef stew,
    canned

oleo / butter

shortening

pancake mix

biscuit mix

bread

flour

cornbread mix

cornmeal

salt pork

steaks

jelly / jam

match safe

common
    crackers

sugar

molasses

vanilla

ginger

maple syrup

olives

pickles

fresh fruit

strawberries /
    strawberry huller

vinegar

oil

hamburg

dish towel/cloth

soaps

potholder

tissue

napkins

towels

candles

scissors

first aid

toilet articles

soft drinks

alum foil

plastic bags

briquettes

tablecloth

ham to fry

fly spray

trail nibbles /
    candy

Plus dishes and pans. If we've left something off, you can do without it for a few days. "First aid" covers a lot; think about that. We do take a deep-fat frier, not just for our potatoes but to oblige a salmon or togue we might fillet, and my reflector oven is good to have (Thoreau called it a Yankee Baker). A galvanized water pail on its side becomes an oven, but don't try a plastic pail. Did I mention a compass? Always have one, and be sure the north end of the needle is marked and you know what the mark means. First day in camp get your bearings and don't forget them, and if you think your compass is wrong, it isn't. It's annoying to think you're approaching Passadumkeag and find yourself in Ste.-Rose-du-Sapin, Quebec. Particularly if you don't know anybody there. The respected rule is that if you don't have something, you can't use it. On the other hand, if you have a reflector oven and don't bake a pan of hot biscuits, the thing will keep your popcorn chummy during the preprandial propitiation exercises. Bear that in mind.

You may wonder about the ginger. That's to liven up the can of Burnham & Morrill baked beans. A dash of molasses or maple syrup, with a touch of baking soda and a pinch of ginger, will make a bland canned bean remarkably cordial.

By the way, in the Thoreau woods of Maine, because they were staple in the lumber camp days, baked beans are called logging berries.

Not only is the cornmeal intended to make a breakfast trout convivial, but a bit of it on your hand when you're filleting a salmon or whitefish for deep frying will render the slippery flesh docile. You have to think of everything when you're beyond Lily Bay.

And never go beyond Lily Bay without a five-gallon can of gasoline and an extra spare tire. And have some U.S. Geodetic Survey maps or some Prentiss & Carlisle maps of the northern townships. They tell you things it's good to know. If you wonder about Indian names, most of them have to do with a squaw dipping water.

Thoreau's wangan included "what we might pick up." Bill and I run no such chance. We take it into the woods with us, and if we don't use it, we bring it out. When we got home last year, I found we still had four cans of Dinty Moore beef stew—one, two, three, and four years old. Next year, five?

THE ALLAGASH RIVER

I feared however that the banks of the St. John were
too much settled. We made this island the limit of our
excursion in this direction.

>   —*Thoreau, at Heron Lake as he decided*
>   *to retrace to Chamberlain Lake and the East*
>   *Branch of the Penobscot*

In the legends of the Penobscot Nation the story of the Creation
varies somewhat from that in our English Bible:

In the beginning, the Great Spirit was void and without form and darkness prevailed. Now and again the
Great Spirit would stir, but inactivity bothered Him and
He longed for something to do. So He rose, and casting
His idleness aside He lifted the mountains from the sea,
set the heavens in place, arranged all the geography, and
created all things that fly and swim and crawl. He set
the Sun and the Moon to divide the days, and after six
days he gazed about to see what He had done, and He
saw that everything was some old good.

Now, He said, this is practice enough, and I have
found out how to do things; let Me spend the seventh
day on perfection and create the finest of the very best!
So on the Seventh Day the Great Spirit did not rest, but
He waved His hands and made Maine's Allagash River.

Just recently (1993) a Maine television station produced a documentary on Henry David Thoreau and his visits to the Maine Woods, and the pictures included some magnificent footage of Chase Rapids—six miles of beautiful white water between Churchill Depot and Umsaskis Lake on the Allagash *River*. Thoreau never saw Chase Rapids. If you want to be strictly tricky, you can say with some truth that Thoreau never saw any of the Allagash *River,* although since his writings were first published (after his death), his name appears just about every time somebody mentions the Allagash *River*. On that memorable Sunday morning the Great Spirit created Allagash Lake, which Thoreau visited and which is in the hills just above the camp at Caucomagomac Lake Dam where Bill and I have frolicked for thirty joyful Julys. From Allagash Lake flows Allagash *Stream,* which descends with pools and rapids and falls, into Chamberlain Lake, where, to all intents and purposes, it ceases to be. Man should not put asunder what God hath wrought, but back before Thoreau's time the lumberers interfered with the arrangements of the Great Spirit of the Penobscots. They dug a channel at Telos Lake so the waters from Chamberlain Lake, and from Allagash Stream, would flow down the East Branch of the Penobscot River. At the same time they built a "lock dam" so no water from Chamberlain Lake could pass, as the Great Spirit intended, into Eagle Lake and then down the Allagash *River,* by way of Eagle Lake. Eagle Lake is now considered the source of the Allagash *River*. Heron Lake, where Thoreau turned back, is a bight, or bay, of Eagle. This distinction with absolutely no difference has caused some readers to suppose Thoreau got lost again (as he did at Mud Pond Carry) and was bewildered in the manner of Daniel Boone somewhere in Kentucky. I think Thoreau knew where he was all right, but like some of his botany, he erred on the good side.

Around 1950 or so there began to appear agitation by nature lovers to "take" the Allagash River waterway and make it into a dedicated preserve. The preservationists kept calling it a virgin forest and an unspoiled wilderness, and

Thoreau's name was invoked frequently to support the argu-
ments. The Allagash Watershed had been logged off repeat-
edly, and at the time of the first national park proposal it was
owned by about a dozen interests. One of the owners was
the State of Maine, which had some reserved lands and also
warden facilities for both Fish and Game and Forestry. All
the owners, some of whom produced forest products and
some of whom owned timberland as investment, partici-
pated in land management with professional foresters. Into
this situation stepped one Stewart L. Udall, a bureaucrat
hatched in the Franklin D. Roosevelt zoo and an Arizonian
who probably never heard of Thoreau and wouldn't know a
basswood tree squeak from a place to dip water. He proceeded in the best New Deal style.

First he got a grant.

Then he fended off the ten thousand patriotic American
foundations which were experts at applying for grants, settling at last on a prestigious consulting firm and poll-taking
society famous for unbiased studies just as soon as you told
them what they were to study and on which side they were
to be unbiased. Folks in Maine soon found how things
trended, and Secretary of the Interior Stewart L. Udall
increased at once in disfavor. The thing got annoying but still
had its funny side. Our forestry commissioner of Maine, at
the time, was Austin Wilkins, a kindly man who knew his
trade and wouldn't lift his voice if a Percheron stood on his
foot. When this expensive and profound "foundation" concluded its studies, and was about to publish its findings,
Commissioner Wilkins remarked that he thought it curious
the fate of such an extensive and valuable asset was to be
decided by a bunch of jerks posing as experts who had studied the Allagash thoroughly without ever going near the
place. The jerks protested this abuse of their scholarly methods, but it was true. Commissioner Wilkins finally sent the
press his letter, ". . . to my certain knowledge, none of the
panel has been on the river."

About the same time one of the Supreme Court justices

who had become a nature lover wrote a book about the great need for the United States to protect its wilderness resources. I think his name was Douglas. He wrote well and was convincing, although more than a few Maine foresters felt he was injudicious in writing about Maine's Allagash when the matter might later come before the Court if Udall kept going. Commissioner Wilkins, whose rangers knew everything, was assured from the wilderness that this judge did spend a weekend at Clayton Lake with some senator whose name escapes me. Clayton Lake has as fine a sporting camp as you'll find in the state. It's several miles west of the Allagash, close to Daaquam, Quebec.

The report of this unbiased survey appeared—a beautiful brochure with ample evidence that only a federal park could save this magnificent Allagash resource from willful destruction by the evil tree-chopping barons of the crass and benighted Maine wilderness. It would bring tears to the eyes of a bird's-eye maple! It did have one flaw that amused every Mainer who saw it. There was an aerial photograph showing the utter devastation wrought to the lovely virgin forest by the tactics of the uncaring chain saw crews who slashed their way and never mind! The picture had been seen rather generally in Maine before, and it was made by one of the landholding companies to include in the stockholders' report to illustrate what a hurricane had done to about twelve thousand acres on Haymock Mountain. There was never such another jackstraw jumble of twisted wood, and the company spent some four seasons salvaging logs before the bugs took over. Blaming mankind for God's carelessness seemed not to bother Udall and his experts. When man clear-cuts a forest, at least he's smart enough to lay all the butts in the same direction.

In the end the plan to nationalize the Allagash River gave way to a plan for state management, and the area today is well managed and well "preserved," but it does lack the advice of trained foresters, who left as soon as private ownership ceased.

Bill and I never heard what became of Udall.

As to the St. John River and its being "settled," Thoreau was correct. Acadians had been there since "the grand dispersal" of the Nova Scotia French—the Evangeline story. The Allagash joins the St. John at Allagash Plantation, and there is no more wilderness. For seventy-five miles "the Valley" is farmland, and then the St. John turns into New Brunswick and heads for the Bay of Fundy.

A COMICAL FOOTNOTE

Some years previous to Stewart L. Udall, the secretary of the interior had been Harold L. Ickes, who was openly called a curmudgeon and relished being hard to get along with. Everybody was supposed to detest Harold Ickes (1933).

Soon after he was sworn into FDR's first cabinet, Harold Ickes decided to make an odyssey and visit all the national parks that were administrated by his department. The place to start would be Acadia National Park down east in Maine with Cadillac Mountain lifting high from the Atlantic Ocean—the seacoast park. Ickes accordingly came by railroad from Washington, without the panoply of official dignity, looking much as any tourist from the Middle West should look, and he sent ahead a telegram to the park administrator that he would like to be met when the afternoon train arrived at Ellsworth; the train didn't go through to Mount Desert Island and the park.

At the park, upon receipt of this message, all was excitement and confusion. Nobody was prepared, and the budget had long since eliminated conveyances suitable for a cabinet member, and the park staff was on a stringent policy—"For gracious sake, didn't Washington know about the Great

Depression?" There wasn't even warning enough so the spare chamber could be scurryfunged and swamped out to oblige a guest! One of the park attendants at the time was a young man, new to the staff, named Wallingford, whose family had lately developed one of Maine's first ski bowls and had introduced "man-made" snow. The lad hoped to apply himself and become a park ranger, for which he had a desire, and he stood at the right place at the right time. He was available to drive to Ellsworth and fetch the secretary, and he did have an available vehicle. True, it was a beat-up Chevy with two mudguards missing, and it skipped on the hills. The muffler was dangling, and the lights didn't light, but it stayed on for personal service because it got thirty-eight miles to the gallon and because young Wallingford knew how to set the distributor so the engine would start.

Wallingford set out for Ellsworth, twenty-one miles away, to meet the train and fetch the Boss.

All went well. Ickes was on time, Wallingford assisted him into the Chevy, and at the park a hastily gathered welcoming committee was ready. Ickes stayed several days.

Wallingford drove him all over Mount Desert Island and prayed the Chevy up Mount Cadillac with great success, and they went over to Schoodic Point and had a lobster feed at Marlboro as well. Wallingford said the secretary was great fun and, as far as he could tell, the exact opposite of a curmudgeon. Wallingford also learned that Ickes was a shark at cribbage. He loved to play cribbage. And so did Wallingford.

That's really how it came about that Ickes asked Wallingford if he wouldn't like to take a leave of absence from his duties at Acadia National Park and drive Secretary Ickes across the country as he made his inspections of all the other national parks. Ickes added hastily, "In my car this time."

Wallingford had a couple of good lines when he'd tell about this. One went, "So I drove Ickes up Mount Cadillac in a Chevy and then drove him up every other mountain in America in a government Cadillac—at just about thirty-eight gallons to the mile."

The other line was "It's true, I suppose, that only two people in history have ever played cribbage in every national
park!"

Which is merely to give me a chance to suggest a cribbage
board and a pack or cards if you venture into Thoreau's
woods and visit the Allagash River. You never know when
somebody you never saw before will say, "Cut for deal!"

SIGNS OF PROGRESS

> The Maine woods differ essentially from ours [in Massachusetts]. There you are never reminded that the wilderness you are threading is, after all, some villager's familiar wood-lot, some widow's thirds from which her ancestors have sledded fuel for generations. . . .
> —*Thoreau, meditating on his way home from Chesuncook, 1853*

Edmund Ware Smith, had he learned to cut his own hair, might have been as fine an authority on the Maine Woods as Thoreau. In one of Ed's books on the oddities of the Matagamon Lakes, he says he dislikes to see any moccasin prints in the wilderness save his own. In Thoreau's time, yes—but Bill and I learned at once to expect bird watchers to step out from the trees at any time, and we became well aware that we were sharing our privileges. Things were not quite like those in Massachusetts—yet—but probably the day is not far off. With the end of the spring river drives and the coming of forest roads engineered for heavy trucks, traffic signs appeared, and while we had to accept them as useful and necessary, they did insert a sour note into the wilderness serenity. Where the road from Lily Bay reaches the Golden Road, a stop sign was erected. Bill and I wondered about enforcing it: The road is not a state highway, the township is not organized, there is no police patrol, and there is no public law setting forth a penalty. Nothing to worry about; everybody stops and looks both ways and has no desire to tangle with a

hundred cords of pulpwood rolling down to Millinocket. At
the same time a few "slow" signs appeared, and some curves
were marked. Also, miles were marked on signs nailed to
trees, each giving its own distance from Millinocket. But not
immediately did directional signs appear.

Well, if you've been in Township 12, Range 6, and you
cross the line into Township 13, Range 6, you won't see too
much difference. It's not like going from Concord into Lex-
ington. Bill and I amused ourselves now and then with
thoughts of some of the signs to be painted and erected when
the Golden Road should be accepted into the Maine turn-
pike system:

WATOOLWANGAMGAMOOK 165 M.

Meantime Julian Allen et Fils had signs pointing to his
camp, and so did some other contractors. Great Northern
had a few signs posting 35 mph. And one day Bill and I were
snug in a bosky dell with our table set for a woodland lunch,
feeling remote and far from the crowd, and a game warden
stepped from the puckerbrush to say good afternoon, boys,
and staple a poster to a tree. He had a real hardware store
stapling machine. The poster said:

FLY FISHING
ONLY

Daily Limit
Five Fish

True, there had always been town line witness posts.
Hewn by an ax and painted bright red, they mark the corners
of townships and are set to stay useful for many years. They
stand six feet tall and can be seen at a distance. They do not
intrude, however, and are acceptable as a wilderness
necessity.

Plenty of souvenirs of the past do intrude. At a lunch spot
we chose at Loon Lake Stream, I cleared space for a fire and

chanced upon a pile of axes in the leaf mold. We presumed
there had been a chopping camp there long ago. The helves
of the axes had rotted away. We were, indeed, in somebody's
woodlot. It was in 1992 that William and I arrived at camp
expecting everything to be about the same and first encountered the bureaucratic arrogance of FERC. This, far from
being out of the past, was strictly of the future, and Bill said,
quoting a line from a play, "I think I'm going to vomit." We
had no idea what FERC was and hesitated to inquire. We
found the answer on one of its signs: Federal Energy Regula-
tory Commission. FERC signs were everywhere, and Bill
and I at once considered becoming a militant group to take
them down and burn them in a demonstrative bonfire that
would bring the forest rangers and their pumps clearn out-
a Greenville.

The log and dirt dam that was still at Cauc Lake when Bill
and I first visited was merely a scenic antique after river driving ceased since there was no further need of "sluicing" wood
from the lake to the stream below. Great Northern laid plans
to replace it with an expensive concrete dam in which the old
sluiceway would be merely a spillway. Holding water, not
driving logs, was the purpose, and that no doubt explains
how the FERC got into the picture. With a fishway and a
spillway, the new dam has four gates to manage the flow of
water as needed. Three of the gates are usually closed in July,
leaving one to entertain the canoeists. Two to a canoe, the
Boy Scouts would be returning from Allagash Lake, and
each canoe would come into position just where the quiet
lake water begins to seethe and swirl for the descent over the
spillway—an angled rush of a couple of rods. Bill and I, just
out of sight at our camp, would be sitting in the afternoon
delight, and as each canoe headed for the spillway, the elon-
gated comments of the Scouts would split the sky and come
to our ears. Good to see city boys having such fun! The boys
who make these canoe trips are given canoe instruction first,
so the descent down the Cauc Dam spillway was not necessarily dangerous, even if the shouts suggested mortal terror.

In the placing of the institute's environmentally acceptable signs, all locations have been approved by the institute's inspector of scenery and the chairman of the Standing Faculty Committee on Niceties. This early site shows the overlook at Lobster Lake, one of Thoreau's favorite spots, and a glance tells immediately how tasteful approach improves an otherwise dull and uninteresting vista.

THE BLACKFLY

However, I finally concluded that the remedy was
worse than the disease.

*—Thoreau as he applied a fly dope near
Mud Pond Carry*

Thoreau's visits to the Maine Woods were previous to the general discovery that vacation fun could be had in the Pine Tree State. Our first invasion was along the coast, where millionaire mansions appeared with forty bedrooms and adjacent bungalows for the servants; Bar Harbor and Ogunquit come to mind. It wasn't until after the Civil War simmered down that "sporting camps" began to flourish on the inland lakes— woodland resorts where a gentleman could retire to angle and later to seek the ponderous moose and the furtive deer, and could book the family for July and August fresh air. Those were the days of trunk vacations, when nobody thought of coming for less than two weeks—by train and steamer.

It was in the 1920s that Governor Ralph O. Brewster invented tourism and added a Development Commission and a Publicity Bureau to the taxpayers' burden. The word "Motel" had not been coined, and all the hotels in Maine were cozy ordinaries of good care and good food dedicated to the comfort of traveling salesmen. Soon lovely old homes along the highways would accommodate tourists overnight at two dollars a couple (no breakfasts!), and Maine had become the Land of Remembered Vacations indeed.

Now it is curious that of all the millions of words that
have been written and published to attract—entice, perhaps
inveigle—the paying customer to our magnificent beauties
and unique pleasures, not one single word has ever brought
the Maine Blackfly out into the open. He remains unsung,
unadvertised. Yet every summercater ensnared has gone
home from his first happy holiday in Maine to speak at
length in Connecticut, in Massachusetts, in New Jersey, in
Philadelphia about nothing else, all winter. Not the rising
sun over Passamaquoddy Bay, not the surging surf at Pema-
quid, not the eager trout at West Branch Ponds, not the
delectable lobster bakes at Bailey Island, not the joys of
unspoiled Katahdin, and certainly not the magnificence of
sunsets from the Molechukemunk overlook at Bemis. It is
the goddamn Maine Blackfly that makes a Maine rustication
memorable.

Thoreau told us that before he set out for Ktaadn, somebody in Bangor gave him a "wash" to apply to keep the
Blackfly and other wilderness insects away, and we realize at
once that Thoreau had no idea why this was such a fine thing
to do for a stranger from the Bay State. Thoreau, still in Bangor, had no notion what the *Simuliidae dipterous* would do to
him when he got to Mud Pond Carry, where he would wade
in a swamp to his knees to learn that in its larval stage the
Maine Blackfly is aquatic and waiting his turn. Innocent,
Thoreau trudged along at the heels of his Indian guide with
his little bottle of "wash" in his pocket, confident in its efficacy. Efficacy, here, means stink.

The Indian didn't tell Thoreau about Blackflies. Thoreau
noticed, however, that his guide didn't use any wash. Indians
had lived with Blackflies for thousands of years and had in a
way become immune. Avoiding soap and water helped. The
tangy abundance of wilderness flavor arising from an Indian
guide in the middle 1800s was basic in the early attempts by
apothecaries to find salves, lotions, ointments, opodeldocs,
palliatives, specifics, and fabrifuges that would render the

paleface as impervious as an unwashed Amerind. I mean no disrespect to my excellent good friends of the Penobscot Nation. Things were that way then, and Thoreau observed that his guide did not use a wash, either in a bottle or in a stream, and was able to endure the Blackflies without.

Now, a word about WOODSMAN. There is a liquid insect repellent available in the stores today with the label " 'Ole Time' Woodsman." It comes in a two-ounce plastic squeeze bottle, bar coded, with the date "Since 1934." It is made by Pete Rickard, Inc., of Cobbleskill, New York, and is further identified as "Pine Scented." It is effective against any of the pests now being considered, but with all due respect to Pete, it is not the WOODSMAN that prevailed in the Maine woods quite some time before 1934.

The story of the origin of WOODSMAN runs about the same whoever tells it. Pete says Obbie Sherer and Doc Don Adams were angling in Maine, and not being immunized in the Indian fashion, they devised a salve that, in effect, made them smell like an Indian. It worked. But evidently Obbie and Doc didn't realize what they had and failed to protect their patent rights, because shortly WOODSMAN could be had in just about every store in Maine, and it was a staple item in every tackle box. In researching WOODSMAN, I asked Ted Wooster, the apothecary in Waldoboro, Maine, what he could tell me about it, and he said, "What do you want to know? I used to make the stuff!" Ted's recollection was that a pharmacist could readily sniff and tell what was in the ointment, and there wasn't any great secret in the formula to be protected. He mentioned a rectified apothecary's tar, citronella, penny-royal, and several other nasties and putrids combined and blended to be the same only different. Ted also felt there may have been a licensing deal, whereby the inventor sold cans and labels and the local druggist was on his own. Joe Bush, a Dexter pharmacist, seemed to remember the original WOODSMAN was made in Monson, but George Wentworth of Monson said no, Monson made spruce gum. Clifford Collins of Freeport, who made pictures for L. L. Bean's early catalogs, has supplied a label from "L. L. Bean's Fly Dope," which Mr. Bean was making in his factory basement and offered well before 1934. When Mr. Bean testified to his customers that he himself used his Blackfly dope "personally," the proof was in his office from ice-out in the spring to just about Thanksgiving. He'd dose himself well with his version of WOODSMAN, go to Goddard Brook for some trout, and return to his office. Blackflies would cease to plague after the first September frost, but any version of the original WOODS-MAN would linger long and lasting. In this way, long before he opened his retail store, Mr. Bean was advertising his fly dope. That WOODSMAN worked was good to know, and that it would gag a skunk had nothing to do with the real purpose. The Flit gun and the Raid aerosol can were refinements that appealed, and Bill and I have never resorted to the real "ole-time" Woodsman. We spray out the camp before bedtime and keep the screen door tight. On field trips we take a Black Flag fogger can along.

There was a device called a kib which was for mosquitoes rather than Blackflies. It was a wooden frame that fitted over a sleeper's head and was covered with mosquito netting. The edge of the netting was tucked under the blanket. A disadvantage was that it got stuffy in there, particularly after baffled mosquitoes settled all over the netting in one last rousing good try. Sometimes we'd see campers using beekeepers' veils against Blackflies, but it gets stuffy in them, too, and the veil is a nuisance if you're paddling a canoe. A smudge, on the other hand, is not an altogether objectionable alternative. Thoreau's Indian made smudges.

A small fire is kindled in a metal pail, and swamp moss and wet pine needles are added to make an acrid, heavy smoke. The pail is placed to the windward of camp, so a light evening breeze will waft towards things. (A stouter breeze will disperse mosquitoes anyway; Blackflies roost at night.) The pungent smoke deters insects, and if the smudge is properly engineered and managed, it is not objectionable. Not unlike a perfumed candle in the royal bedchamber, meant to soothe the cares of the day and knit the sleeves of Ravel. But take things all in all, and Thoreau was right: You might's well take the fly bites as put up with the treatment.

One version of WOODSMAN, about 1910, was made in Little Compton, Rhode Island, and it was already designated as "old-time." The two-ounce can sold for thirty-five cents, and it stunk about fifty dollars.

One spring, long ago, Flint Johnson and I walked in to Spencer Stream by the Joe Pokum Bog trail, and we were using a new kind of fly dope called 6-12. It was said to be compounded of buckwheat sap, would deter biting insects, and had no offending smell. It was working all right in that respect, but the vehicle of the liquid, whatever it was, rubbed off our hands and made the varnish on our fly rods gummy. Later we had to rub down our rods and refinish them. But Flint and I didn't stink like WOODSMAN.

We got a nice snatch of trout, and at that time Spencer Stream had never been stocked from a hatchery, and ours were all original, native, Spencer Stream trout. A beautiful fish, more silvery than not, and with brighter spots. We found a couple of handy rocks where we could sit and watch the purling tumble of a pool where a trout would rise to entertain us from time to time. I opened the lunch basket and distributed nourishment, and Flint said, "By Moses! That's the best corned beef sandwich I ever introduced my teeth to!"

I said, "My kitchen chef always corns her own brisket, to get it just right."

Flint said, "She's too good for you."

Then he stood up and sniffed, and he said, "We got company!"

"I didn't hear anything," I said.

"Oh, you wouldn't hear them; they're still two miles up the trail."

"*They?*" I said. "Come, come, my dear Mr. Sherlock Holmes, explain your deductions!"

"Elementary, my dear Doctor Flotsam," he said. "WOODSMAN, and it's two strong for one and not strong enough for three. They approach upwind, and they'll be here in twenty minutes."

So Yves Nadeau and Leo Potvin came swinging along, and by that time I could smell the WOODSMAN, too, and above the head and shoulders of the two were swarms of Blackflies keeping their distance. Flint knew the boys, so they found rocks and had sandwiches, and that's just about all I can tell you about WOODSMAN.

FOR RAINY DAYS

> . . .an odd leaf of the Bible, some genealogical chapter
> out of the Old Testament, and, Emerson's address on
> West India Emancipation; also an odd number of the
> Westminster Review for 1824, and a pamphlet entitled
> History of the Erection of the Monument on the Grave
> of Myron Holly.
>
> —*Reading matter Henry Thoreau found
> in a lumbermen's boomhouse at Quakish Lake,
> thirty miles from a road*

The first time Bill and I stayed at the Great Northern dam tender's camp at Caucomagomac Lake, a shelf in the southwest
corner was bowed downward by 282 copies of *Reader's
Digest*. That figures to over twenty-three years. On the first
rainy day I conducted an unbiased study of the *Reader's Digest*
editorial technique and found that any given "Illustrative
Anecdote" is repeated every forty-two issues, or in three and
a half years. On the following twenty-nine revisits, which
bring us up-to-date, Bill and I brought sufficient reading
matter to cover rainy days, and of a quality to stimulate our
cultural desires. In 1987 somebody mercifully cleaned house
and began using the shelf for storing canned fruits and vegetables. Other than the *Digests*, reading matter left (by others)
in camp ran to *Penthouse, Playboy,* and a Canadian magazine
called *MacLean's.* There were always daily newspapers, well
out-of-date, but kept for starting the woodstove in cooler
weather.

In our State of Maine a person of unfriendly tendencies, one who is hard to get along with, is often rated as one you'd like to have in camp on a rainy day. Of all the words used by Mainers to mean exactly the opposite, that's the champ. One who has never experienced a rainy day in the Maine Woods will never force his imagination to realize what it is like. First is the awful realization that this is not what you came for. Then you begin to sort out the differences. An overcast sky will usually invite the fish to play, but a real rain will "drive them down" and strikes are unlikely. Besides, no matter how much rain gear you've brought, you soon find a thwart in a boat or canoe is the wettest place in the world. A stroll in the pristine forest? Red Johnson liked to say, "I get no hilarity under a spruce tree in the rain." Every well-ordered woods camp will have a cribbage board, but after ten or twelve games monotony sets in. Flip Carver once guided a sport on Eustis Ridge, and the day it began to rain during breakfast the sport dug a cornet out of his duffle, perched on a chair so the horn pointed at Crocket Mountain, and he blew until Flip grabbed the cornet and wrapped it around a birch tree. It is easy to undersand why 282 copies of *Reader's Digest* were embalmed and treasured up for rainy days. On rainy days, after walking from window to window and looking out at the rain from each, any scholarly person will find himself reading the ingredients on a Bisquick package.

The middle week in July, which was usually the time Bill and I sojourned, has a good average of pleasant weather. We got, over the years, a few afternoon thundershowers, some at night, and very few rainy days. Knowing it would be a rainy day in camp, we'd adjust readily, and after washing the breakfast dishes, we'd turn to literary pleasures. A couple of times the rainy-day temperature would be cool enough to warrant a fire in the ancient Wood & Bishop ram-down stove, and after the heat came we'd pop some corn and open a can of mixed nuts. Bill's taste for camp reading was heavier than mine; he liked history and biography and always had some heftier magazines. I found rainy days in camp were great for embracing again all manner of worthy books I'd read in the long ago. It was great joy one year to find Wilkie Collins again. I did have a couple of Dickens things with me but found out all over again, after such a long time, that I still preferred Collins. For three years running I took in my two-volume edition of *Gil Blas,* and we didn't have a drop of rain. But the next year we had a two-day northeast blow, and with *Gil Blas* I was happy and glad.

Neither Bill nor I read in bed, but on rainy days we'd shift our chairs from the windows over under the gas-mantle propane lamps our camp had, and after supper we'd put a new music tape in our player and continue our literary program until bedtime.

I have been careful to tell this to prevent a public presumption that all Bill and I did on these outings was play around and waste our time. Unlike Thoreau, who botanized the dandelions and then passed quickly along to further scenery, Bill and I wrought great scholastic good on the many days we were moving about. We never shunned our obligations to introduce the finer things into the vast wilderness, dividing our efforts equally among the seven liberal arts and sciences.

Dr. Dornbusch's development of the Universal Robot is a case in point. Very early in our series of visits to the forest lands of the Great Northern Paper Company, we realized that the antique methods and techniques of harvesting timber needed to be upgraded, and after a study and report by an unbiased panel of experts, the Caucomagomac Dam Institute of Fine and Coarse Art funded a program and named Dr. Dornbusch director. After a full year of close application, Oskaar, the all-purpose robot, was demonstrated with great success. Explaining that Oskaar could be programmed to perform any task, great and small, and shut itself off when the work was completed, Dr. Dornbusch set the robot to harvesting ten acres of prime spruce in the institute's experimental woodlot behind the new girls' dormitory. In the process, new seedling trees were cloned to the stumps as each tree was removed, so the forest became self-perpetuating within minutes. Instead of transporting the logs at great expense and with complicated machinery to the distant mill, the fiber was converted to a vegetable essence and sealed in twelve-ounce cans, to be taken to the mill by a boy on a bicycle. One can of this essence, when reconstituted, made wood fiber sufficient to operate the mill for ten months. An academic forester from the University of Maine, visiting our institute, said, "It's incredible! I don't believe it!" Dr. Dornbusch explained that a mere ten acres of timberland, thanks to the cloning process, would keep the Great Northern Paper Company competitive in its field, and the rest of the corporation's wilderness could be developed into house lots, donated to the Nature Conservancy, set aside for rubber raft enthusiasts, marked off for bird-watching, and reserved for all types of mobile homes. After this demonstration the robot prepared a delicious roast beef banquet for the invited guests and later entertained them with selections from Brahms and Mozart on the Scottish Pipe, accompanied by the Poland Pond steam zither concert band.

At an equally successful scientific convocation in 1987, the Department of Dracontology of the Cauc Dam Institute released its report on the existence of Cauco, the Caucomagomac Lake Monster, which had hitherto been considered a myth like the Loch Ness Monster, the Champ of Lake Champlain, and the Memphree of Lake Memphremagog. Recent efforts to establish the authenticity of such monsters by pictures and soundings had been inconclusive, and those directed at Memphree were dismissed as spurious by scholars. Knowing that Cauco, the resident monster in Lake Caucomagomac, was indeed real and had a nest on an abandoned boom pier just off the institute campus, the institute provided a grant and invited numerous savants to assist in the verification.

It was quickly established that Cauco did exist and was incubating. Cauco was a fish-eating saurian, classified as "landlocked." It was ascertained that both sexes alternate on the eggs and also that in off time each fishes at the lake end of the fishway, or ladder, in the new Cauc Dam. This resulted in a visit from a Maine game warden, who read the general angling law to Cauco and his mate, warning that fishing within 150 feet of a fishway is illegal. These instances, along with so many others, indicate the many ways the institute has advanced learning, and particularly understanding, in the upper townships. The institute takes pride in its accomplishments towards the uplift of the uninhabited acres beyond the influence of customary facilities. And at no cost, either by voluntary contribution or imposed tax on the fortunate folks who benefit from the many advantages.

The good Bill and I have accomplished leads us to feel we have repaid in some measure the gracious favors we have enjoyed. And not only that, we are not wasting our time just because we have a rainy day. To steal a thought from the eminent English poet Wordsworth:

> Yet, helped by Genius—untired Comforter,
> The presence even of a stuffed Owl for her
> Can cheat the time.

Anything helps, and you must have something.

LE TEMPS DES SUCRES

The civilized man not only clears the land permanently
to a certain extent, and cultivates open fields, but he
tames and cultivates to a certain extent the forest itself.
—*Thoreau, thinking on his Maine
Woods*

Henry David Thoreau did mention the maple trees in his writings about the Maine Woods but said nothing about making maple syrup and maple sugar. Neither did he mention maple sweetening when he mentioned sugar and molasses. So the great maple syrup production of the North Woods must have developed after his time, and it is a fine example of the way civilized man tames and cultivates the forest that in another way, he can spoil. William never came over to Maine from Vermont in *le temps des sucres* to see how the Maine Woods turn out a great deal of Vermont maple syrup, but in our July visits he did see the great sugar "orchards" in the St. John River valley, where tens of thousands of sugar maples are tapped every March and April to prove that men do use the forest without harming it.

Along the International Paper Company road from Ste.-Aurélie, Quebec, to our tent site at Baker Lake, certain leases of sugar maples are made every spring to Canadian citizens along the border. This has been going on since just about Thoreau's time and has become very much hereditary. Leases go to the same families year after year, and only when a family does not renew is a *sucrerie* available to be leased to a new family. These "sugaries" are in that category of places "You can't get to from here." North of Greenville the roads drift with winter snow, and if you want to visit one of these sugaries in season, you'd best go up to Canada and come back into Maine at St.-Zacharie, St.-Philibert, Ste.-Aurélie, St.-Juste, and Daaquam. Now you will find all the sugar cabins open, families in residence, and everybody hard at work deriving the precious *sirop d'érable* before the spring bursts and the season is over. It is, of course, strictly a French-Canadian effort, and while it is entirely in Maine, is has no logical connection with downstate, and hardly any Mainers know it goes on.

An explanation often advanced is that these are people who are needed to some extent in the operation of Maine's working forest, so the timberland owners are smart to give them some work in the off-season. As soon as the maple season is over, they will become truck drivers, choppers, cooks, and their families will return to Quebec. The "fee" for the privilege of working a *sucrerie* in Maine is completely a token—a cent or two for each taphole into which a spile or *andouille* is inserted to direct the sap into a pail or a tube. Usually the timberland people let the Canadians count their own holes and take their word for the number. Otherwise, it is the job of a company scaler to count tapholes, a piddlin' job every scaler feels is far beneath his dignity. A scaler we talked to at Ste.-Aurélie explained his strategy. He said when the season was begun and everybody had his spouts in place, he'd pass the word along that "tomorrow" he was going to show up and begin counting. Immediately about half the *sucriers* would hurry in and pay up, explaining that they had just counted again and found they had twenty-three hundred more spouts than they supposed. In this way Scaler Miranda spared himself much work and kept everybody honest. Some of these operations run to many thousands of trees. One man told Bill and me, "I'm just a little fellow; I have only twenty-four hundred pails."

Bill hasn't, but I have been to a sugarhouse in that region during the sap run. During the week the man and wife and their always numerous children attend things, and sap is allowed to accumulate for attention on the weekend, when all the uncles and cousins and boyfriends and girl friends, visitors (and sometimes paying guests!) and no doubt the parish priest come to help out and join in some ceremonial festivities. Food is traditional: a shoulder or ham, with roasted potatoes, a pot of baked beans, hot biscuits, crepes the size of a stove lid, and a general overpowering of maple syrup—everything served within the steam from the monster-great evaporator. Maple syrup is ready to "draw off" at 220° F. The high spot in the sugarhouse meal is "sugar eggs," which are cooked in the evaporator by the master *sucrier*. Break as many eggs as are desired in a big bowl, froth them as if for scrambling, but no milk, and dump them into the steam of the "front pan." The eggs are well cooked before they ever touch the hot syrup. Retrieve them with a skimmer, leaving them enough half-ready maple syrup to create an abundant flavor, and a batch of sugar eggs are eaten before they get three feet away from the source. A sugarhouse party in Maine is just like those they have in Quebec.

To counteract the constant sweet-sweet-sweet of a sugarhouse party, "Ears of Christ" are a delicious must. When I first heard of *les oreilles de Christ,* I thought it was a flippancy, but I soon learned the term is used devoutly. Strips of salt pork are fried to near crispness in the big frying pan, and the heat quickly twists them into a curl that suggests the shape of a human ear. The French-Canadians are strong on salt pork *(lard salé)* in their cookery, but after so much maple sweetness the Ears of Christ serve to neutralize things and, I suppose, get you ready for more crepes soaked in hot syrup. When you drive away from a *partie de sucre* in the brisk frost of an April evening in far-up Maine, you will find, as you get to your motel in St. Georges, back in Quebec, that your mittens have stuck to your steering wheel—a sugar-sweet reminder that you have just experienced the greatest!

As the maple syrup is made, it is stored in sixty-gallon steel drums to be picked up later for transport to market. At the time I visited the sugaries near Ste.-Aurélie, not much, if any, of the Maine-made syrup was credited to Maine. It went into Quebec's Beauce County to be lost in the grand total of Canadian maple products. It was tested and graded by Canadians under Canadian standards. Much of it came to be stored in a warehouse in Sherbrooke, Quebec, operated by the Boudreau Brothers. I suspect much of it was held in escrow by banks acting for buyers—to be delivered in lots as needed for manufacturing. The Boudreau Brothers did the delivering, and down at the Derby Line, upon entering Vermont, the Boudreau Brothers discreetly became the Bowdry boys. Some, but nobody knows just how much, of the Maine syrup is blended in Vermont to become a Green Mountain product. I always tell Bill, "The best part of it!" When the Golden Road was completed and the big maple forest along the St.-Zacharie border was opened, several new sugaries were set up—terrific enterprises with oil-fired evaporators and miles upon miles of plastic tubing. The spiles and the pails and the gathering tanks are eliminated, but once a week the plastic tubing must be flushed out by a gasoline-powered pump and brook water to remove a natural vegetable residue the old-time sugar people never knew about.

FALSE PREMISES

> Wild as it was, it was hard for me to get rid of the associations of the settlements. Any steady and monotonous sound, to which I did not readily attend, passed for a sound of human industry. The waterfalls which I heard were not without their dams and mills in my imagination,—several times I had been regarding the steady rushing sound of the wind over the woods beyond the rivers as that of a train of cars. Our minds, everywhere, when left to themselves, are always thus busily drawing conclusions from false premises.
>
> —*Thoreau, meditating along the East Branch, 1857*

One lunchtime Bill and I fell into a chat with a gentleman in lavender shorts at the Boomchain Restaurant in Greenville, and he said he was "stopping" at the Spencer Bay Camps and had come into town to pick up a few things and look at the dry flies in Sanders's Store. Bill suggested he try a How Now and a Brown Cow, and the gentleman thanked him happily. I could see that the good care and attention I had been giving Bill over the years were beginning to pay off, and in time he might "become one of us." You go into the woods, and you come out of the woods. And after shopping you go out from town and back into the woods. Bill said the lavender pants alerted him, but it was the "into" that made his ears snap.

Thoreau did well with this small distinction, and if a bunny thumped his heels in joy in yonder bushes, he may have thought the postman was at the door, but he soon recovered and said, *"Lepus americanus virginianus!"* The tendency to confuse urban and wild land matters is far from limited to going into the woods. Bill and I heard of a woman who came out of the woods one time and continued to think she was still in. She was a respectable lady, wife to an MIT scientist, and she and her husband had been on the Allagash River for three weeks. At first she had wandered from false premises, as had Thoreau, but instead of thinking the rustle of the wind was the swift passage of the Halifax Express, she was more practical and would feel along the tent wall for a light switch. But then after a week she was altogether in the woods.

Then she came out of the woods. They brought the canoe ashore at the village of St. Francis on the St. John River, packed their gear, and by arrangement somebody would come tomorrow to take them home to Massachusetts. That afternoon they walked the few steps into (they were out of the woods now) St. Francis village and took a room in a tourist home overnight—their first bed in going on three weeks. All in the dark, that night, the lady, drawing a conclusion from false premises, awoke, rose from bed, and thinking she was still in the tent stepped a discreet distance and wet all over the bedroom floor.

Maine is loved by a great many well-meaning, sincere folks who like to leave their snug "associations with the settlements" to come into our Maine Woods and become devout disciples for what ails us. They are eager to save our scenery and fresh air for generations to come. We must do something! We must do something while there is yet time! There are people who hear a cock o' the woods at his carpenter work and suppose a jackhammer is repairing a water main. The porcupines plighting their troth in the top of yonder pine do, indeed, sound like subway wheels squealing on dry tracks at Park Street Station. There are people, not all of them in lavender pants, who look at the piles of limbs and decry the clear-cut as the last felonious assault on God's great, green, beautiful forest.

Bill and I don't see it quite that way. We have seen the new trees, trim, tall, and eager, crowding skyward at the Ragmuff lot. We know Maine has been cut off, is being cut off, and will be cut off again. The stewards of the Maine wilderness are the professional foresters whose job is to keep the mills in wood. There is certainly a false premise about preaching one way and then hustling home to read a newspaper—or a funny book. Thoreau made this distinction: "I like better the surliness with which the wood chopper speaks of his woods, handling them as indifferently as his axe, than the mealy-mouthed enthusiasm of the lover of nature." Which, of course, does not mean all lovers of nature are working from false premises. But there, now! Bill and I mustn't moralize!

When Earth's last picture is painted and the tubes are twisted and dried, and the last Man stumbles into the abyss of oblivion, what shall we do to be saved? The statues of the heroes will fall in the dust, and the skyscrapers will rust away. Then God will certainly admit with a wry smile that He goofed that time. And aeon upon aeon afterwards, when God feels it is time, He may select a small flibbertigibbet of possibility and command it to rise and replenish the Earth— just to amuse Himself and see what happens this time. Fish, flesh, fowl, microbe—what might it be? (Please, God—must it be Man again?) And so one day a new life will appear, and all that time the Maine Woods will have been renewing itself, and the trees will be straight and tall, each after its own kind, and the moose will flourish and the beaver slap his tail, and the running waters will be sweet and pure. Man and his ax, Man and his motorboat, Man and his roads, Man and his preservations—nothing of him and them. Just the real old woods as they were before they were used and abused, and loved and admired. God will take notice, again, that they are good. And maybe another time Bill and I can find some way to get, once again, to Baker Lake and Caucomagomac Dam.

ACKNOWLEDGMENTS

To all who, over thirty years, helped Bill and me to understand and love our great North Maine Woods, our thanks are profuse. My first Great Northern friend was Bob Hume, and since his time a succession of woodland executives has added the personal touch that makes a great corporation like Great Northern amiable and warm. Some are mentioned already, but let me speak of John Maines, Jim Giffoon, Charlie Nelson, Jim Perz, George Therrien, Henri Marcoux, Bob Bartlett, Bun Bartley, Bart Harvey, Dick Morrison, Frank Morrisette, Warner Nutter, Ed Blodgett, Paul Firlotte, Ralph Currier, and our present custodian of the institute's endowed funds, Tom Wildman. Who'd I forget?